The Divine Intruder

The Divine Intruder

When God Breaks Into Your Life

JAMES R. EDWARDS

WIPF & STOCK · Eugene, Oregon

THE DIVINE INTRUDER
When God Breaks Into Your Life

Wipf & Stock
An Imprint of Wipf and Stock Publishers
199 W. 8th Ave., Suite 3
Eugene, OR 97401

www.wipfandstock.com

PAPERBACK ISBN: 978-1-4982-9742-4
HARDCOVER ISBN: 978-1-4982-9743-1
EBOOK ISBN: 978-1-4982-9744-8

Manufactured in the U.S.A.   MARCH 6, 2017

To Janie

mulier fortis et constans

for her strength and constancy

Contents

Preface

BOOKS, LIKE INDIVIDUALS, HAVE gestation periods that, although unseen by readers, determine their lives. This book began as a series of talks that I delivered in church and conference settings around the country in the late 1980s and early 1990s. I transformed the talks into the chapters herein and sent the manuscript to a number of publishers, none of whom found it a proper fit. The academic houses generally found it too popular, and the trade publishers thought it too demanding of readers. I had ceased sending the manuscript to publishers and virtually abandoned hope of its publication when NavPress senior acquisitions editor Don Simpson blew the cold embers of the manuscript to life and published it in 2000 under the title, *The Divine Intruder: When God Breaks into Your Life*.

It is my distinct pleasure to see *The Divine Intruder* welcomed back into print again by Wipf and Stock Publishers. Except for a minor editorial changes the present reprint preserves the identical text of the edition published by NavPress. The new cover, however, better illustrates the dynamic nature of the Divine Intruder who breaks into our world in order to bring people into fellowship with himself and service for his kingdom. Also new in this edition are "Questions for Discussion" appended at the end of each chapter. I wish to thank Sharon L. Reidenbach for assistance in drafting the questions, which I hope will be stimulating and edifying for readers, especially in groups. Finally,

I thank Drew Spainhower at Wipf and Stock for initiating and successfully piloting the republication of *The Divine Intruder*.

There is a tantalizing likeness between the history of this book and the stories I write about in it. Like Abraham and Sarah and Moses, to whom the promise of God seemed lost and forgotten, a surprise appearance of the Almighty rekindled a dormant hope and made its fulfillment possible. The publication of a book is, of course, not of the same magnitude as the birth of a child in Mary's case or the deliverance of a people from slavery in Moses'. But surely the magnitude of an event is not as important as the divine intervention itself which, whatever form it takes, signals the fulfillment of God's promise to make all things new.

James R. Edwards
Spokane, Washington, 2017

Introduction

THIS IS A BOOK about conversations. Even though conversation has fallen on hard times in our day of rapid-fire data transferral and breezy talk shows, the ability to sustain a dialogue on a subject of consequence still remains one of the essential and (for me at least) most satisfying arts of life. The conversations in this book share all the properties common to conversation in general, with the major exception that one of the partners is God rather than a fellow human being. Thus the subject of this book is conversations with God. That might suggest a book about prayer, but only one of the conversations in this volume has anything specifically to do with prayer. The conversations in this book, rather, are more like the direct, no-nonsense talk you might hear between a coach and players in a locker room before a game, or from a teacher helping a student solve a problem, or between two lovers attempting to express their love for one another.

The Bible, as most everyone knows, teaches us about God, but it does not often teach about God *didactically* — in the way, for example, that a survival manual teaches one how to tie knots and avoid hypothermia and locate the points of a compass. At least it teaches this way less often than people suppose. The Bible is rather a history of God's dealing with our world, and as such it is a record or story. We discover who God is by his relationship to us and our world more than in straightforward metaphysical or ethical instruction. One of the ways God relates to our world is in speech, some of which takes the form of actual conversations or dialogues between God and humans. I have selected eight such conversations, all direct discourse between God (or sometimes a messenger of God) and a human partner. My objective is to consider these conversations as paradigms of the way God deals with our world, not just in biblical times, but still today.

Some of the characters are sterling examples of the ways we should like to talk and respond to God. Mary's response at the Annunciation, for instance, is a model of humility and trust. Likewise, the story of Jesus in Gethsemane, although not without Promethean struggle, is the clearest window into the soul of our Lord and his self-sacrifice for our fallen world. But most of the characters are much less heroic. As a rule they receive the call of God with reluctance and doubt, or resist it outright. Some are hesitant and evasive; most are frightened and alarmed; a few are cowardly; and one even declares he would rather die than obey God.

And what of God? God is the tireless initiator who calls his human counterparts to the risk of faith, with all the challenges and fears and joys that entails. But God's profile is less definable and more elusive than the profiles of his human partners. The human responses to God can all be classified according to various categories, but God's character never fully escapes the realm of mystery. God possesses authority, but God is not authoritarian. God expresses his will concisely and unambiguously, yet God is not dogmatic. God holds the rudder unswervingly to the point of destination, but God is not dictatorial. God, in other words, is distinctly unlike our caricatures of him as a smothering, autocratic, arbitrary, removed, or even nonexistent deity. God is solid as granite, but that does not relegate his human counterparts to the status of impressionable wax figures. On the contrary, God's solidness encourages, even demands, thicker blood from the human side. God permits his human allies to work through the implications of his momentous inbreaking into their lives, like a fisherman who plays a fish that is bigger than the test of his line. The conversations are therefore much more than an exchange of words. In many of them the actual dialogue is cropped and, in itself, of less than dramatic proportions, lacking the fleur-de-lis quality of genteel conversation. Nevertheless, despite the lack of sophistication, each conversation is probing and determinative, expressing the uncompromising wills of both parties. The human partners resist, but God persists and eventually prevails.

The ancient Jews developed a method of expounding Holy Scripture for its historical, linguistic, and theological significance, but equally for its contemporary relevance and application. Both the method and the resultant volumes of interpretations or commentaries are known as *Midrash*. The word comes from a Hebrew root meaning "to inquire of, investigate, or search out"—with God frequently as the object of the inquiry. What I attempt in the following chapters might be called *Christian Midrash*. The interplay between the historical and contemporary—what it was like then, how it might look today—is a fascinating and fruitful tension that is, in my view, the only proper subject of anything deserving the name of theology. If some readers, especially those trained in academic theology, are surprised at my occasional stepping down from the seat of objectivity in order to illuminate ancient texts through contemporary and even personal illustration, I shall be the first to admit that I do this because I believe the Bible is every bit as much God's word to us as it was to its original readers. Despite the disfiguring of God's image in both ourselves and the world around us, this is still very much God's world, and everyday life, as witnessed to in literature and history and certain personal experiences, continues to reflect, however imperfectly, not only the truths revealed in Scripture, but its leading Character. It is my hope that the illustrations I have included will serve that purpose.

There have been occasions in my life, as I am sure every reader can recall in his or her life, when a particular conversation brought me to a new plane of reality. Some years ago when I was in Tübingen I paid a visit to Professor Ernst Käsemann, one of the living legacies of German theology. He reminisced about his long and eventful life—his place in the "Tübingen school," friendships with the makers of twentieth-century German theology, participation in the Confessing Church that opposed Hitler, and his role in the formation of German democracy after World War II. Past events and personalities returned to life in the octogenarian. The past was no longer a disparate sequence of meaningless events but a chorus of voices from different times and places, woven into a harmonious whole in Käsemann's memory. During the conversation Käsemann and I ceased being two atomized personalities. A meeting had occurred in which we had tapped a wellspring or felt a pulse that extended beyond the normal limits of time and space. Life seemed to surpass itself and, if only for a short while, the normal was suspended and transcended by something greater.

We are told that Moses' countenance once radiated glory after meeting with God (Exodus 34:29). Even in an entirely human conversation I had experienced something of the mystery of the eternal and transcendent. As I walked down the street after meeting with Käsemann, I had a feeling of invincibility. *Not even a bullet could stop me,* I thought to myself. The Jewish philosopher Martin Buber helps us understand this mystery of encountering the other. One of Buber's lasting insights is that "All life is meeting."[1] In that disarming statement, Buber affirms that relationships — the encountering of another individual as a *thou* — give true meaning to life.

This is true not only, or even primarily, in human relationships, however. Christian thinkers have long taught that human speech, and hence human conversation, is an echo or stammering of a preceding divine conversation. Conversation is indeed one of the indelible marks of our being made in God's image. Conversation must entail at some point an articulation in and exchange of words. It is no coincidence that one Person of the Trinity is known as the *Word.* In my understanding as a Christian, the meeting of which Buber spoke is thus a reflection, however distant, of the very nature of the Trinity, and it includes the meeting that comes about through language. The Trinitarian God invented meeting, and grants it to humanity. The Trinity is a community — a communal unity. The Trinity is like an ensemble in opera in which Father, Son, and Holy Spirit sing three different motifs but produce a harmonious whole; three singers, one song, each delighting in the voice of the other, each contributing to the dominant melody. Dante, creator of *The Divine Comedy*, the greatest epic poem not only of Christendom but of Western culture, expressed this trinity not as sound but in terms of form and color in the Beatific Vision, "three circles, three in color, one in circumference; the second from the first, rainbow from rainbow; the third an exhalation of pure fire equally breathed forth by the other two."[2]

The meeting of God and humanity is one of the leitmotivs of Western art up to the time of the Enlightenment, which crested about the time of the founding of the American republic. An interesting depiction of the encounter of the terrestrial and the celestial is Caspar David Friedrich's *The Cross of the Mountains*, located in the Charlottenburg Palace in Berlin. The painting is dominated by a sharp and barren mountain peak projecting through a sea of clouds below. On the summit of the mountain is a man hanging on a cross, toward the foot of which the solitary figure of a woman veiled in diaphanous garments approaches. Apart from the crucified one and the woman, there is no life in the picture—no one else on the angular summit, no animals, no trees or vegetation, no town or village in the valley below. Elevated and sublime, the cross supersedes the world and is entirely separated from it.

The crucified one, of course, is intended to represent Jesus, but he is in fact small and distant and not the focal point of the painting. The focal point is rather the woman, whose translucent garments and immateriality surpass time and space. Her ethereal form—combined with the lack of secondary detail in the painting—symbolizes the lonely ascent of the soul to God.

The Cross of the Mountains awakens in many viewers, I suspect, a sense of and perhaps even a wistfulness for the eternal and infinite. Although the painting was produced in 1811, its evocative depiction of the quest for transcendence speaks powerfully to the wave of interest in spiritual phenomena in our own day. We have learned from experience, however, that "spirituality" is not an automatic good. It can be either a blessing or curse, depending on its motives and results. If it leads to a meeting with the true God, then it is, of course, a gateway to eternal life. But not all roads take us to our desired destinations, and not all spiritual quests lead to God. If pursued to wrong ends or in wrong ways, such quests can lead us further from grace, not closer to it. Friedrich's canvas is a case in point. The subject of the painting is not, in fact, Christ or God, but the divine quest of the intrepid human soul as symbolized by the woman. The transcendent and eternal in the painting are essentially a point, not a person; the goal of the soul's quest is a destination (or perhaps the journey to it), not a meeting with the living God.

The painting is thus the precise opposite of God's encountering of us and our world as revealed in the Bible. The Bible does not present the epic of the human search for God. When we open the Bible, the Israel we read about is not in search of God, nor is Abraham or Gideon or Deborah or Paul or the apostles; even the prophets, whose consciousness of God exceeds anything we know from any culture in history, are reluctant recruits. These and other characters in the Bible are all going about their own business, the first order of which was much the same then as it is now. In those days it was to fit in with the nations round about; today it may be to fit in with the crowd, make the grade, or join the party. Into the drama that they have scripted for themselves, God breaks in.

The Jesus of history did not hang above the world in an ethereal and disembodied state. He dragged a heavy cross through the dank streets of Jerusalem and was crucified on Skull Hill as Roman soldiers staved off the tedium of duty and as dice throwers and gawkers milled about. Perhaps in rare moments we fancy ourselves, as Caspar David Friedrich's painting suggests, storming the summits of virtue or "getting religion" or encountering the Infinite. But who has ever made good on the resolve to reach the summit? Alone in our hospital rooms or prison cells or dorm rooms; in the long years of middle life when the road seems to stretch endlessly before us; in our battles with greed, lust, vice, mediocrity, boredom, resignation, and cowardice; when we feel trapped by a job or a town or a marriage or a temperament, we realize that without the inbreaking of God and his saving word from beyond ourselves, our lives would lack any meaning at all and degenerate to smallness, insignificance, and, for many, something frightening. The God of the Bible does not draw intrepid souls upward to the Olympian heights. Nor can God be found by concentrating our powers and plumbing the depths within. God does something far more unsettling: he breaks into this world, even when he is unexpected and unwelcome. God joins us in our weakest and worst moments. Every character in the following pages testifies to that. The world is not a safe place after all, if by safe we mean safe from visitations of the Holy One. There is a Divine Intruder among us.

1

Disillusionment with God

The Lord appeared to Abraham near the great trees of Mamre while he was sitting at the entrance to his tent in the heat of the day. Abraham looked up and saw three men standing nearby. When he saw them, he hurried from the entrance of his tent to meet them and bowed low to the ground.

He said, "If I have found favor in your eyes, my lord, do not pass your servant by. Let a little water be brought, and then you may all wash your feet and rest under this tree. Let me get you something to eat, so you can be refreshed and then go on your way—now that you have come to your servant."

"Very well," they answered, "do as you say."

So Abraham hurried into the tent to Sarah. "Quick," he said, "get three seahs of fine flour and knead it and bake some bread."

Then he ran to the herd and selected a choice, tender calf and gave it to a servant, who hurried to prepare it. He then brought some curds and milk and the calf that had been prepared, and set these before them. While they ate, he stood near them under a tree.

"Where is your wife Sarah?" they asked him.

"There, in the tent," he said.

Then the Lord said, "I will surely return to you about this time next year, and Sarah your wife will have a son."

Now Sarah was listening at the entrance to the tent, which was behind him. Abraham and Sarah were already old and well advanced in years, and Sarah was past the age of childbearing. So Sarah laughed to herself as she thought, "After I am worn out and my master is old, will I now have this pleasure?"

Then the Lord said to Abraham, "Why did Sarah laugh and say, 'Will I really have a child, now that I am old?' Is anything too hard for the Lord? I will return to you at the appointed time next year and Sarah will have a son."

Sarah was afraid, so she lied and said, "I did not laugh."

But he said, "Yes, you did laugh."

—Genesis 18:1-15

A BRAHAM IS SITTING IN the doorway of his tent at midday, thinking. He wishes his life had turned out differently. A sinking disillusionment settles in his stomach as he realizes that he is old. The ideals and hopes of earlier years have passed him by.

According to custom older than memory itself, he has positioned his tent a few paces away from the trade route. The place is Hebron, a caravan junction where a few oaks huddle near the west side of a plain surrounded by a semicircle of hills. Northward, in the direction of Damascus, is Abraham's birthplace, Ur of the Chaldees. To the south lie Beersheba and the Sinai desert. Abraham is looking not to the north or south, however, but to a point not found on the compass: he is looking to the past.

For the ten-thousandth time, he is pondering the ways of the Almighty. Abraham had become a wanderer late in life — not because he was a nomad in the true sense of the word, but because he believed God had called him to such a life. Compared to cosmopolitan Ur, the places he now frequented — Hebron, Ziph, Gerar — were as nothing. Never would he have chosen such a desolate existence had he not a burning conviction that his migration to Canaan was God's will. In his younger years, perhaps, the prospect of sojourning in Canaan might have held a certain fascination for him. But in his mature years, his wanderings were the result of obedience to a divine imperative rather than a choice on his part. For reasons that were no longer clear — if they ever had been — Abraham's life had taken turns quite at odds from what he had once been, from what he would have chosen. To receive a great name, to become a great people, to inherit a great land — this was his and Sarah's destiny.

Or rather, that had been their destiny, withered now by long years of unfulfillment. In bitter moments, Abraham doubted whether the Almighty had called him at all, perhaps even whether the Almighty existed. But whenever he replayed his life's story as he now did from the doorway of his tent, the presence of God was there.

Undeniably, his destiny was not his choice but God's promise, made before he ever set foot on the mountains and valleys, the crags and oases of Canaan. Still, the terrible dilemma of faith remained. Could Abraham trust the promise of God that kept repeating itself in his existence, or would he succumb to the obvious evidence of his own advancing age and Sarah's inability to bear children?

His experience was a riddle. It was like coming to an impasse in a maze, or groping in the dark for something that could not be found. The riddle was the more perplexing because in everything the Almighty had been faithful . . . except in the one thing that mattered most: the birth of a son, an heir to the promise. Abraham and Sarah could surely be forgiven if on occasion they had resorted to scheming in order to help God make good on his promise. Sometimes it seemed that they, mere mortals, might be more effective in fulfilling the promise than the Almighty. What could be wrong with meeting God halfway? With proposing Eliezer, steward of Abraham's house, to fulfill the role of a son, for example? Or with Abraham's fathering a child through Sarah's maid, Hagar? But all their stratagems failed, for God was intractable and would accept no surrogate sons. The impasse of God's unfulfilled promise loomed ever before Abraham and pushed his faith to the brink of despair. From the doorway of his tent, how perilously close faith and despair seemed.

It was to a man with such thoughts that something extraordinary happened: "The LORD appeared to Abraham near the great trees of Mamre while he was sitting at the entrance to his tent in the heat of the day." To Abraham, it appears that he must resolve the bitter ironies of life on his own. But there is more to faith than is apparent to Abraham's mind. He is not alone. A visitor is at hand, even if the exact identity of that visitor at first escapes him.

To be sure, it was God who appeared to Abraham. God's appearance, however, has nothing to do with Abraham's hospitality. Nor is Abraham's meeting with God something he has conjured up; it is not the result of a momentous resolve on his part, much less a scaling of the ladder of mysticism. He is simply an elderly man with an elderly wife who has tried as best as he could to be obedient to his understanding of God's will.

But it is not God whom Abraham recognizes. Looking up, he simply sees "three men standing nearby." Where had they come from? Has Abraham been so lost in thought that their approach across the lonely expanse has escaped him? It is not normal—or safe—for a Bedouin to be taken by surprise. Before he knows it, they are standing before him, expecting to be received. And nearly as suddenly, Abraham is on his feet, as much from consternation as from hospitality, bowing low in honor and defenselessness before his guests, allaying any suspicions of hostility on his part. "If I have found favor in your eyes, my lord, do not pass your servant by," responds the patriarch. No sooner said, he arouses the camp in a fever of errands—the fetching of water, curds, and milk, the preparing of cakes and bread, and the slaughter of a young calf from the herd.

God's appearance in the form of Three Strangers raises the curtain on the greatest act of the divine drama—the incarnation, or enfleshment, of God in human form. The act will reach its climax in Jesus of Nazareth, but from the outset of the biblical record there are hints or foreshadows of it. From time to time we are told that the Director steps onto stage himself, although seldom in a leading role. More typically it is a quite insignificant part—here, three unnamed strangers; much later, a carpenter from Galilee. God *incognito*—God in disguise—is one of the recurrent surprises and mysteries of biblical faith.

At age fifty-one, well after he had become a renowned novelist, Leo Tolstoy was converted to a simple, practical form of Christianity. Following his conversion, Tolstoy plumbed the essence of the teachings of Jesus in a number of short stories. One of the best known, "What Men Live By," is the story of a hard-luck Russian couple who, quite against their will, take a naked stranger into their primitive dwelling in the dead of winter as a last resort against his freezing to death. The money the husband Semyon earns as a cobbler scarcely provides for their needs, no matter how sparing his wife Matriona is. Another mouth to feed is the last thing Matriona needs.

Surprisingly, however, the circumstances of the couple begin to change. The stranger becomes Semyon's apprentice, and the fame of the new apprentice spreads quickly, as people come from great distances to have shoes and boots made by him. Indeed, the stranger brings more than prosperity to the impoverished dwelling. What began as a reluctant duty on the part of the couple to save a man from freezing becomes to them a blessing. They receive more from the stranger than they have given to him. They have learned "what men live by"—not by material goods, but by the love of God. Suddenly, a flash fills the room and, like Abraham, Semyon sees that the stranger is not a mere mortal after all. The one whom he and Matriona have taken in and clothed and fed is, in fact, an angel sent from God.

Like Semyon, Abraham is at first unaware of the nature of his guests. To be sure, in most translations Abraham addresses the Three as "my lord," as though he recognizes God in them. But this overinterprets the Hebrew *adonai*, which often is—and certainly is here—a simple honorary epithet, "sirs," or "gentlemen." Nevertheless, from the outset it is apparent that the Three are no ordinary wayfarers. "Where is your wife Sarah?" they ask. "There, in the tent," Abraham replies. Then the strangers say, "I will surely return to you about this time next year, and Sarah your wife will have a son." The veil of Abraham's ignorance is beginning to fall, for the strangers know too much. How do they know Sarah's name, or that she is childless and that she and Abraham wait in vain for a son? Abraham and Sarah stand not on holy ground, but in holy company. Indeed, together they are part of the holy company, for what God has to tell them they cannot hear separately. God's word to Abraham includes Sarah, and God's word to Sarah includes Abraham. Each needs the other to hear the word.

The word that comes to them, however, stretches their faith to the limits of absurdity. "I will surely return to you about this time next year," says the spokesman of the Three, "and Sarah your wife will have a son." This exceeds the realm of human possibilities, and Sarah erupts in laughter from behind the tent flap. How can she and Abraham expect to give birth at their age? The future is closed to them, determined by the hard facts of biology. That much is clear to Sarah, who knows well enough when women are past childbearing age. And yet it is precisely the impossible that they are asked to believe. The word of God comes to this aging couple as anything but a reasonable act.

In July of 1988, I stood on an elevated platform at Potsdamerplatz overlooking the Berlin Wall. I had just returned from my sixth visit to churches in East Germany. My first visit to East Germany had been in 1965, just four years after the Wall was erected, and my visits in the intervening years had established and deepened friendships with pastors and congregations throughout the Communist-dominated eastern sector. Never had I met more vital believers or engaged in more intense and satisfying conversations than I had with Christians in East Germany. But in July of 1988, my heart was sullen and heavy, for conditions in the East were at a nadir, and Christians I had known for years were fatigued and desperate. I had mounted the Potsdamerplatz overlook in order to pray for my brothers and sisters in the East before returning to America — but as I looked at the garish graffiti on the Berlin Wall, and beyond it to the desolate no-man's land and the gray bank of East German high-rises on the horizon, a wave of resignation overcame me. I recalled the opening lines of a book I had read years before: "I cannot say when the Wall will be breached. I cannot forecast when reunification will come. I can only state my firm conviction that the Wall will be dismantled in a meaningful period of contemporary history. . . . The Wall will come down and Germany will be reunited."[1] What naïve and mocking words those seemed as I gazed on the impenetrable concrete barrier before me, and the defense perimeter, rigged with machine guns triggered by laser beams, behind it. *This cursed Wall will still be here when my grandchildren come to Berlin,* I said to myself.

A little over a year later — in about the same amount of time, in fact, that the Three Strangers had promised a child would be delivered by Sarah — that seemingly irrevocable scene changed. The exact reasons and causes of the Fall of the Wall on November 9, 1989, are not entirely clear, but one thing is clear: the Berlin Wall fell, and it fell remarkably similarly to the prediction of Eleanor Lansing Dulles in her 1967 book, *Berlin — The Wall Is Not Forever.*

What a lesson I learned about not foreclosing on the promises and power of God. How similar my sardonic resignation at Potsdamerplatz was to Sarah's mocking laughter behind the tent flap. Yet it is precisely at crisis points like these that the question of faith haunts us, just as it haunted Sarah and Abraham. She and Abraham must decide whether their future is determined by their circumstances or by God. They can do one of two things: They can opt for hard-bitten realism in the face of their hollow prospects, give up the promise of God, and laugh at the preachers of unseen realities as cruel tricksters. Or, they can choose to trust that God's word to them is not a trick, but truth. If — just if — this word is true, then faith is the hardest thing in the world, for it calls us to give up our very lives — including our well-reasoned arguments and excuses — and hold fast to the only word that speaks to our deepest longings in life.

God knows Sarah's struggle behind the tent flap. The laugh is heard, to be sure, but so is the torrent of disappointment and bitterness behind it. Surprisingly, God responds not with a rebuke — well enough deserved, perhaps — but with a question on which Sarah's existence hangs: "Is anything too hard for the LORD?" Despite everything, can Sarah trust God? Nearly two millennia later another woman, although younger than Sarah and unmarried, would receive a message in a hill town of Galilee that she would become the mother of the Messiah. In Mary's struggle of faith, God would repeat the same sentiment: "For nothing is impossible with God" (Luke 1:37). Jesus himself would warn his disciples not to tether God to their narrow expectations, but to allow God to be God: "Nothing will be impossible for you," he said (Matthew 17:20). This, of course, does not mean that *everything* is possible. It means that everything that is *promised by God* is possible, exactly as we are told, "so that the LORD will bring about for Abraham what he has promised him" (Genesis 18:19).

The question drives Abraham and Sarah to the bedrock of existence. It leaves them reeling, and they react to it differently. Abraham, the consummate Bedouin host, scurries around like a solicitous waiter; he is dumbstruck, as if too despairing to respond. Sarah, who until now has been unseen and unheard, laughs rudely . . . followed by a righteous protest that she did not laugh. "Yes, you did laugh," says the Holy One. Quivering on the threshold of faith, Abraham and Sarah are typical of believers of every age. Contrary to popular opinion, the astonished couple is not a model of belief, but of disbelief.

After Abraham and Sarah's years of anguish, how utterly anticlimactic this one-liner: "I will surely return to you about this time next year, and Sarah your wife will have a son." Their very existence has been gnawed away by the futility of such hope. Suddenly, unexpectedly, nonchalantly, Three Strangers drop the news. And no sooner has the announcement been made than, according to the Hebrew, they arose and departed as unexpectedly as they came. Abraham and Sarah had done their duty as hosts supremely, but it was not they who served their guests. It was the guests who served them with the promise of a son to a barren couple. They received a message of hope in a time of abandonment. True, the old patriarch was caught flat-footed, and his wife could not contain her incredulity. But fortunately, not everything depended on their response. Had their response been the deciding factor, the Three Strangers would have shaken the dust from their feet and looked for more faithful company elsewhere. But human resistance is not the last word. Where Abraham and Sarah falter, God seizes the baton and, in majestic soliloquy, repeats the promise that Abraham will become a great and powerful nation, a blessing to the world.

It is an unspeakable consolation to know that salvation de- pends on God, not on our faltering faith. Not that Abraham has shown any lack of faith; until now he has demonstrated remarkable fortitude, first in putting forth Eliezer's name as his successor in order to help God fulfill his promise of a son. When that overture was rebuffed, he took Sarah's mistress, Hagar, hoping to raise up an heir from her. Entire epochs of Christian history have been defined and dominated by the stuff of these chapters. Who makes the first move in the divine-human encounter? Is it up to Abraham to take the first step, or is it God who takes the first step? Some schools of thought argue that the human partner must take the initial step of salvation apart from divine assistance. Had not Abraham done that? How easily the chosen couple might be regarded as necessary partners in fulfilling the divine commission. But all talk of "humanity playing its part" or that "God helps those who help themselves" is now shown for what it really is, a pitiful attempt at self-justification. Abraham and Sarah's reserves are exhausted, their hopes dashed. They stand not before a bright and promising future, but before *no* future—a blankness, nothingness. They are like a prisoner who has been denied his last reprieve, who now stands irrevocably before the gallows. How rightly the apostle Paul spoke of their plight as "deadness" (Romans 4:19).

Abraham may have thought himself alone in the universe. He may have been tempted to conclude that the death of the promise spelled God's absence or even death. But this Abraham did not do — or God did not allow him to do. In the visit of the Three Strangers, God had broken into Abraham's experience at a critical moment, renewing his call and rekindling the hope of an heir. The persistence of grace has a way of interrupting our eulogies at the gravesides of the impossible.

Several years ago when I was on sabbatical in Germany, I received a curt and dismissive rejection of an article I had submitted for publication to a theological journal. I had, of course, received rejection letters before — every author has. But this article, submitted to a leading journal in the field, summed up several years of doctoral work, as well as my aspirations as a scholar. I have never considered myself prone to depression, but the rejection of what I considered my calling was worse than a threat to bodily existence. I was swept into a vortex of doubt and despair. As I walked through a nearby woods in gentle snowfall, I felt as though I were gazing into hell itself. Hell was not terror — it was nothingness, an utter void. I had no idea if I even believed in God, in meaning, in life. A few days earlier I had prayed that I might die to self and live fully and freely for God. Could this be God's answer? If so, it was a sentence I could not bear. My life seemed to me a terrible burden. Rather than defending my work, I found myself siding with those who rejected it. I felt a loathing and contempt for myself, wanting to complete the work of destruction on myself that had been wreaked on my manuscript. I felt like Naomi, the biblical character who changed her very name because God had dealt harshly with her. I recalled Abraham trudging up Mount Moriah to sacrifice his son. But God had arranged for a ram to be substituted for Isaac at the last minute. God had made no such provisions for me; my firstborn, as it were, was killed. My footprints in the snow seemed to lead to an abyss.

For several days I was as immobilized as a statue carved in stone. Our children, however, had winter vacation from school, and earlier I had promised to take them sightseeing over the break. Out of a sense of duty, I kept the promise. In a certain village, my wife was taking the children on a tour of a beautiful baroque church. I was standing alone by the main portal. As I waited, I glanced at a nearby literature rack. There was a poem in German by Rainer Maria Rilke, which I translate as follows:

> When something is taken from us,
> With which we are deeply and wonderfully bound,
> Much of ourselves is also taken away.
> It is God's will, however,
> That we find ourselves again,
> Richer, despite all our loss,
> Multiplied, despite unending pain.

Those words seemed, like the Three Strangers, to know too much of my circumstances to be coincidental. That night I wrote in my diary, "Is this God's word? Is this true for me? I'm afraid to believe and hope. God, help my unbelief."

I believe the words of that poem, like the visit of the Three Strangers, were a "humble" miracle of God. God is in the business of blowing the dim coals of faith to life—in Abraham and Sarah, and in you and me—and he does so in unexpected ways. The very banality of the closing words of Genesis 18 after the Lord and Abraham have concluded their conversation remind us of this mundane mystery. The original Hebrew reads, "Abraham returned to his place." After all Abraham and Sarah have experienced, how do they "return to their place"—to bleating flocks, disgruntled servants, tents needing repair, then; to unpaid bills, blaring televisions, and the frantic chase of modern life, now? Perhaps it was not as banal and anticlimactic as we might suppose, for it was not in mystical transport, or in an out-of-body experience, or on a mountain top that God had revealed himself to them, but "in their place"—as Abraham sat in the doorway of his tent pondering his perplexing sojourn in the outer reaches of Canaan, as Sarah hovered between hope and despair behind a tent flap. Within a very ordinary place, something very extraordinary happened. God broke into their resignation and disillusionment with an unsolicited overture of promise and hope.

And how did God break in? Some people say ruefully, "God doesn't talk to me like he talked to Abraham." Perhaps we have said it ourselves. Perhaps we even doubt that God speaks to us at all. It helps to recall that Abraham and Sarah did not see God. They saw what appeared to be only three strangers. The later narrator of the story recognizes the appearance of the Three as an appearance of God, but at the moment Abraham and Sarah do not see it so. God is often present when he is least recognized. Centuries later, a grieving woman at a tomb looked at the resurrected Jesus—right at him—and mistook him for a gardener (John 20:15). God's habit of appearing in disguise prompted early Christians to exhort one another: "Do not forget to entertain strangers, for by so doing some people have entertained angels without knowing it" (Hebrews 13:2). Cannot we, like the narrator of the story, look back on our lives and see that a telephone call, a chance meeting, a letter, an unexpected visit, a misfortune or unanswered prayer—yes, even a poem in a literature rack—was Three Strangers in our lives, unrecognized at the time, but God incognito?

And so Abraham returns to his place. The place is the same, but Abraham and Sarah are not. The Divine Intruder has done in them what he has done in Sarah's womb—new life has been generated where sterility and death were foregone conclusions. The promise of a son—crucial as it was to guarantee the future— also sustains Abraham and Sarah from despair in the present. That is one of God's greatest—and most common—gifts: the gift of hope to keep us in the game, to return us to our places not as the same people we were before, but awake, alive to God's transforming presence in our midst.

QUESTIONS FOR DISCUSSION

1. What do Abraham and Sarah teach us about faith?

2. Why would a loving Father "stretch" Abraham and Sarah to the breaking point?

3. Attempting to do things for God is normally considered praiseworthy. Why is it that in Abraham's and Sarah's case God considers it disbelief?

4. Describe your emotional journey while waiting for God: disappointment, disillusionment, or doubts?

5. Can you look back and see God in disguise in your life and circumstances?

2

Contending with God

Jacob sent messengers ahead of him to his brother Esau in the land of Seir, the country of Edom. He instructed them: "This is what you are to say to my master Esau: 'Your servant Jacob says, I have been staying with Laban and have remained there till now. I have cattle and donkeys, sheep and goats, menservants and maidservants. Now I am sending this message to my lord, that I may find favor in your eyes.'"

When the messengers returned to Jacob, they said, "We went to your brother Esau, and now he is coming to meet you, and four hundred men are with him."

In great fear and distress Jacob divided the people who were with him into two groups, and the flocks and herds and camels as well. He thought, "If Esau comes and attacks one group, the group that is left may escape."

Then Jacob prayed, "O God of my father Abraham, God of my father Isaac, O LORD, who said to me, 'Go back to your country and your relatives, and I will make you prosper,' I am unworthy of all the kindness and faithfulness you have shown your servant. I had only my staff when I crossed this Jordan, but now I have become two groups. Save me, I pray, from the hand of my brother Esau, for I am afraid he will come and attack me, and also the mothers with their children. But you have said, 'I will surely make you prosper and will make your descendants like the sand of the sea, which cannot be counted.'"

He spent the night there, and from what he had with
him he selected a gift for his brother Esau: two hundred
female goats and twenty male goats, two hundred ewes
and twenty rams, thirty female camels with their young,
forty cows and ten bulls, and twenty female donkeys and
ten male donkeys. He put them in the care of his servants, each herd by itself, and said to his servants, "Go
ahead of me, and keep some space between the herds."

He instructed the one in the lead: "When my brother
Esau meets you and asks, 'To whom do you belong, and
where are you going, and who owns all these animals in
front of you?' then you are to say, 'They belong to your
servant Jacob. They are a gift sent to my lord Esau, and he
is coming behind us.'"

He also instructed the second, the third and all the
others who followed the herds: "You are to say the same
thing to Esau when you meet him. And be sure to say, 'Your
servant Jacob is coming behind us.'" For he thought, "I will
pacify him with these gifts I am sending on ahead; later,
when I see him, perhaps he will receive me." So Jacob's gifts
went on ahead of him, but he himself spent the night in
the camp.

That night Jacob got up and took his two wives, his
two maidservants and his eleven sons and crossed the
ford of the Jabbok. After he had sent them across the
stream, he sent over all his possessions. So Jacob was left
alone, and a man wrestled with him till daybreak. When
the man saw that he could not overpower him, he touched
the socket of Jacob's hip so that his hip was wrenched as he
wrestled with the man. Then the man said, "Let me go, for
it is daybreak."

But Jacob replied, "I will not let you go unless you
bless me."

The man asked him, "What is your name?"

"Jacob," he answered.

Then the man said, "Your name will no longer be
Jacob, but Israel, because you have struggled with God
and with men and have overcome."

Jacob said, "Please tell me your name."

But he replied, "Why do you ask my name?" Then
he blessed him there.

So Jacob called the place Peniel, saying, "It is because I saw God face to face, and yet my life was spared."

The sun rose above him as he passed Peniel, and he was limping because of his hip. Therefore to this day the Israelites do not eat the tendon attached to the socket of the hip, because the socket of Jacob's hip was touched near the tendon.

Jacob looked up and there was Esau, coming with his four hundred men; so he divided the children among Leah, Rachel and the two maidservants. He put the maidservants and their children in front, Leah and her children next, and Rachel and Joseph in the rear. He himself went on ahead and bowed down to the ground seven times as he approached his brother.

But Esau ran to meet Jacob and embraced him; he threw his arms around his neck and kissed him. And they wept. Then Esau looked up and saw the women and children. "Who are these with you?" he asked.

Jacob answered, "They are the children God has graciously given your servant."

Then the maidservants and their children approached and bowed down. Next, Leah and her children came and bowed down. Last of all came Joseph and Rachel, and they too bowed down.

Esau asked, "What do you mean by all these droves I met?"

"To find favor in your eyes, my lord," he said.

But Esau said, "I already have plenty, my brother. Keep what you have for yourself."

"No, please!" said Jacob. "If I have found favor in your eyes, accept this gift from me. For to see your face is like seeing the face of God, now that you have received me favorably."

—Genesis 32:3–33:10

ENCOUNTERING GOD. IT IS an elemental need in our lives. One of the early church fathers, Augustine of North Africa—a great sinner who became a great saint—said this as he reflected on his life: "You have made us for Yourself, O God, and our hearts are restless until they rest in You."[1]

God has made us for himself. That being the case, the longing for God is not limited to Christians, or even to religious people. True, we manage with surprising success to live without God most of the time. As long as we are conducting business as usual, our fronts serve us well enough. But let a crisis befall us, and cracks inevitably appear in our veneers of self-sufficiency. When the telephone rings and brings news of tragedy, or when the bottom falls out of things, like drowning victims we flail for help beyond ourselves. I once was climbing a rock face in Colorado when my partner, who was on the rope below me, unknowingly thrust his hand into a wasps' nest in a cleft in the rock. The wasps swarmed him and he was stung perhaps a dozen times before letting go of the rock. As he peeled off, he cried, "O God!" I arrested his fall with my belay, but he began to swoon from the stings and I had to assist him in a rappel off the face. In a circumstance like this, "O God" falls from our lips as readily as the air we breathe. And surely this is not a vain use of God's name. It is often true that a crisis lays bare the bedrock of our lives.

In one way or another most of us want to encounter God. We want to know God's name and character, hear his voice, even see his face. But our desire to know God usually carries a qualification with it. Most of us desire to meet God — in any significant way, at least — only in times of crisis. When things are going well we do not feel a need for God, nor do we think much about God or hope to meet him. Success and prosperity usually lead to complacency rather than to spiritual sensitivity. No one prays for the second coming of Christ on his wedding day, or on the night of the prom or retirement banquet. But let a hailstorm wipe out your crops, or your family fall apart, or a scandal befall you, and suddenly God becomes a stronger option. In times of desperation there is no limit to which people will go to reach God.

Jacob was at such a point in his life. He had been in crises before, but not like this one. In the past his craftiness and quick footwork had succeeded in sparing him the consequences of his actions. Always before, he simply moved on and hustled a living elsewhere. At least it had turned out that way when he bilked his witless brother out of both his birthright and blessing. What a performance that had been! Isaac, the father of Esau and Jacob, had sent the elder Esau to prepare food especially as he liked it from the wild game of the fields. While Esau was gone, Jacob and his mother Rebekah cooked up a recipe of their own. Rebekah quickly prepared a pair of goats to Isaac's taste; Jacob pulled on Esau's clothing, covered his arms and neck with goat hair, and impersonated his elder brother before his father. No matter that Jacob did not look like Esau: the simulated smell and feel of Esau could be relied on because of Isaac's failing eyesight. And no matter that cheating an elder brother out of his father's blessing was a shabby thing to do: Esau had already forfeited his birthright to Jacob, and for nothing more than a bowl of goulash. Surely there could be nothing very wrong about depriving someone of something that meant little to him in the first place.

The ruse worked fabulously: Isaac was snookered, and Jacob made off with his brother's birthright and blessing. True, the escapade had infuriated hairy Esau, who was much tougher than Jacob, and Jacob had to flee northward to Haran to his uncle Laban. But even there he had managed enviably well. In less than fifteen years he had married not one, but two, of Laban's daughters, and acquired their two mistresses as well. The four women had borne Jacob a dozen children. And from a small portion of Laban's herds Jacob had amassed a bleating-and-braying stockyard of sheep, goats, camels, cows, and donkeys. Jacob's success in Haran, although less objectionable than his dealings with Esau, had a similar effect on Laban as his chicanery had on his brother. When Jacob pulled up stakes from Laban's digs, relations between uncle and nephew were strained.

How we Rationalize!

And so Jacob is on the move again. There is nothing new in that—except that this time he is not moving on. He is heading back—to a rendezvous with his past. And Jacob's past is not something he relishes meeting. When we do shabby things, we often assume that once they are done they will fade away and cease to be. This causes us to think of the past in abstract terms as something unrelated to the present. Yet the past is not something disjointed from the present, but of a continuum with it, part of a *living* history of relationships—either honored or broken. Like furniture out of place in a familiar room, we often bang our shins into it if it is not in the right place. Jacob's past is worse than a room full of misplaced furniture, however. His past is on the move—and not just coming to meet him, but tracking him down. His "witless" brother is marching toward him—with four hundred men!

Sometimes God meets us from out of our pasts. One of the most memorable events of the 1989 fall of the Berlin Wall was a little-known episode related to Erich Honecker. Honecker, who had been general secretary of East Germany's Communist Party since 1971, exceeded most of the Communist bosses of other European satellites in ruthlessness and repression. Although Honecker had not himself built the infamous Berlin Wall, he had succeeded in transforming it into a state-of-the-art technological wonder, and he managed, along with the world's most sophisticated spy apparatus, to create a virtual prison of East Germany. One of Honecker's cabinet members was his wife Margot, who was in 1989 the minister of education in East Germany. Christians had never been granted equal educational opportunities in East Germany, but under Margot Honecker's doctrinaire Communism they were forbidden all access to university education.

In October 1989 the winds of freedom were blowing strongly in East Germany and in other European Communist regimes. In an attempt to shore up its dwindling power, the Communist Party of East Germany deposed Honecker. The stratagem was short-lived, for three weeks later the Wall was breached and forty years of Communism in East Germany were history. Following their ouster, the Honeckers became pariahs in a land they had ruled like monarchs. They were despised by the people they had oppressed and shunned by politicians and political parties vying for power.

Heeding Christ's command to love his enemies, a devout Lutheran pastor named Uwe Holmer took the Honeckers into his home and fed them from his table. His eldest daughter, who had been denied a university education by Margot Honecker, vacated her bed for the couple to sleep in. The Honeckers found themselves face to face with persons they had treated with utter contempt, dependent for their very survival on "elements" they had reckoned as expendable pawns. The Honeckers refused to bow their heads when grace was said at meals, or even to express thanks when they fled the country two months later; and though they recognized it not, in pastor Holmer's family the former East German despots were seeing the human face of God.

Jacob was in for a similarly fateful rendezvous with his past. Like the Honeckers, Jacob was suddenly at the mercy of one he had despised. But God was preparing Jacob to respond to his past in a way that the Honeckers were not prepared to respond to theirs. The imminence of Jacob's encounter with Esau reached to a new depth of Jacob's character, or perhaps *produced* a new depth of character in him. Jacob was greatly frightened and distressed, we are told. For the first time in his life Jacob does something different with his fear and entrapment. He turns to God, entrusting his way to God's sovereign and inscrutable purposes:

> O God of my father Abraham, God of my father Isaac, O Lord, who said to me, "Go back to your country and your relatives, and I will make you prosper," I am unworthy of all the kindness and faithfulness you have shown your servant. . . . Save me, I pray, from the hand of my brother Esau, for I am afraid he will come and attack me, and also the mothers with their children. But you have said, "I will surely make you prosper and will make your descendants like the sand of the sea." (Genesis 32:9-12)

It is a remarkable prayer, and doubly so coming from Jacob. We have not seen such a spirit in Jacob before. The change, ironically, is brought about not by God's censure, deserved as that would be, but by God's lavish and undeserved grace.

Augustine's stormy life again provides a parallel to Jacob's. Shortly before his conversion, Augustine, fully aware of what he must do to follow God's will but afraid he did not have the strength or will to do it, imagined chastity personified as Lady Continence assuring him thus:

> Can you not do what these [Christians] do? Do you think they find the strength to do it in themselves and not in the Lord their God? It was the Lord their God who gave me to them. Why do you try to stand on your own strength and fail? Cast yourself upon God and have no fear. He will not shrink away and let you fall. Cast yourself upon him without fear, for he will welcome you and cure you of your ills.[2]

That is the assurance Jacob pleads for at the Jabbok, that God will provide the strength to do what he calls him to do. It is the first glimmer of honesty and humility, the first glimmer of longing for God's purpose that we have seen in this shellacked schemer. For the first time, Jacob acknowledges someone other than himself as the source of his good fortune. For the first time, Jacob confesses his need for a resource beyond himself. For the first time, he prays that God will save him, not just condone or prosper him.

Jacob's tenderness at the Jabbok is surprising, but it does not alter his being Jacob. True to character, he has a plan in mind. He divides his family and flocks into droves, sending the servants with the flocks first, followed by his family, with himself last. The gift of flocks and herds and the sight of defenseless women and children—perhaps these will atone for Jacob's wrongs against Esau and soften his heart, if it can be softened at all.

The author of Genesis then includes a phrase that would be wholly inconsequential were the subject anyone but Jacob: "Jacob was left alone." We have not seen Jacob alone before. Aloneness and solitude can work wonders in someone like Jacob who has

spent his life trafficking in the affairs of others. Then night fell . . .
not only on the land, but on Jacob's soul. In the lonely stretches of
darkness, when sleep fell on all but this troubled soul, the inescap-
ability of Jacob's fate engulfs him. He knows not how to describe
the nature of the conflict. At first it appears that the contest will be
waged on a human level—frightening, to be sure—but perhaps
still winnable. "A man wrestled with him" is all he is conscious of.
How often truly spiritual battles mask themselves, at least initially,
as mere mundane matters. Under attack, Jacob fights with dogged
determination until the hours of darkness are consumed. He is
unflagging in his resolve to prevail over his assailant, whoever he
might be.

But somewhere in the interminable conflict Jacob becomes
aware that his struggle is not merely a human contest. Perhaps it
never had been. Perhaps it is not a human adversary with whom
Jacob is wrestling, but God himself. But if God, then it is a very
mysterious God, for this God makes himself vulnerable to Jacob's
blows, limiting himself to the measure of Jacob's strength. Seizing
the handicap of his inscrutable opponent, Jacob cries out, "I will
not let you go unless you bless me." That exclamation touches a
nerve within us, does it not? Jacob is beyond the saccharine religious respect that we are taught to display toward God. He is no
longer playing by the rules. His desperation throws him into head-
on contention with God. Like a boxer in the fifteenth round, dead
tired and forgetting all his coaching, Jacob strives with every ounce
of life for God's blessing.

God, however, is no pushover, no matter how determined
Jacob may be. Nor is God a divine rubber stamp who accommo-
dates our every wish. Even within his self-limitation, God remains
God. "What is your name?" he asks. God plunges an inescapable
question into Jacob's heart. This is a hitch in Jacob's hope—and
ours—to meet God. In ancient Israel, names were not coincidental
labels as they generally are today. They were bestowed, rather, to
designate the essence of one's character. A name was not simply
something you were called; it was a description of who you were.
When the Stranger asks Jacob's name, he is asking Jacob to divulge

who he is—his character, heart, and substance. And that moves Jacob—as it moves us—beyond our comfort zone. We prefer to know God's name. We want a God we can call on to meet our needs, but we hope it will not be necessary to go into much detail about ourselves. It is safer and more convenient if the controls are in our hands. On occasion most of us are willing to use others for our own ends and pleasures—and we are not above using God likewise.

But God does not allow himself to be so used. God is in control. It is he who determines the outcome of the struggle. God asks Jacob his name, and in revealing his name Jacob must make a confession, for in Hebrew Jacob means "overreacher," "someone who tries to get more than he has coming," or "someone who skirts issues rather than facing them." Jacob has lived up to that name—and then some. In telling God our name, we have to reveal who and what we are. It is, quite literally, a prelude to the Last Judgment, when every thought and deed must be defrocked before God. That will be a day of red faces and hung heads; but even knowing God now demands something like it. It means dropping our sham defenses and our self-serving justifications and surrendering to the one who knows every crack and crevice of our lives, yet accepts and loves us. Jacob must make a crucial disclosure at the ford of the Jabbok. He is, in fact, at the ford of life, for until he acknowledges who he is, he cannot see God, much less his brother Esau.

It is hard to decide who was the more remarkable contestant in this desperate struggle: Jacob, in his indefatigable determination to overcome; or his divine opponent, who seemingly allowed himself to be overcome. We cannot ignore the mysterious role in which God cast himself in this contest, for it reveals a deep truth about the divine nature. We can only marvel at God's humility. The Hebrew word translated "wrestle," *ahvak*, comes from the root word for "dust." A wrestler was someone who was willing to roll in the dust with his opponent. That is the level to which God condescends to meet Jacob. God wrestled with Jacob not to destroy him, however, but to transform him. The divine combatant entered the fray with this fitful scion of the patriarchs not to wipe out his name, but to give him a new one—and following the name, a blessing. In the midst of the struggle the human partner found that his name was changed from Jacob, "one who deceives," to Israel, meaning "one who strives, perseveres, or exerts oneself."

When I was a freshman in high school I went out for the wrestling team. I succeeded in making the team because I was the only boy small enough to wrestle in the 95-and-under weight division. Among the schools we wrestled was a school for deaf and blind students. As the smallest wrestler, I wrestled first. My opponent was a boy who was blind, and I vaguely recall the referee instructing me in center mat that it would be necessary for me to tie up with him to begin the match. (The normal way of beginning a wrestling match is by "tying up": each wrestler grabs the back of the neck of his opponent with his right hand and holds the right elbow of his opponent with his left hand. This draws the wrestlers head-to-head and ear-to-ear, giving a blind person the feel for his opponent's position.) I was very nervous, and despite the obviousness of the referee's instruction, it did not fully register with me. When the bell rang, I quickly ran around my opponent and tackled him. The next thing I was aware of was the referee tugging on my shoulders. He interrupted the match and repeated his instructions. "Son, you must remember whom you are wrestling. Your opponent cannot see. Unless he can hold onto you, you have an unfair advantage over him." This time I understood. I went out on the mat, tied up with my opponent—and he defeated me.

God deals with Jacob much like the referee admonished me. God remembers with whom he is wrestling. He ties up with Jacob as a way of limiting his advantage. Israel literally means those who "tie up" with God, just like a wrestler ties up with his opponent. So significant is this contest that Jacob becomes the prototype of Israel, which forever after will bear his name.

> In the womb [Jacob] grasped his brother's heel;
> as a man he struggled with God.
> He struggled with the angel and overcame him;
> he wept and begged for his favor. (Hosea 12:3-4)

To be called by this God, to be an "Israelite," is thus not to be a completed character, not to have a perfected faith, but to be in a wrestling match with God. This may seem a rather impious description of faith, but it is a most accurate biblical description of faith. It is only in his struggle with God at the Jabbok that Jacob is assured of the unfailing commitment of God's grace, the pledge of God to struggle and persist with him until he becomes like God.

The contest at the Jabbok is thus not only a dark night of the soul; it is a transforming encounter for Jacob. There are striking ironies in this tug-of-war between God and Jacob as there are whenever we ourselves meet God. Jacob has succeeded in wresting from God the desire of his heart—but not without cost, for in the process he suffers a dislocated hip. The outcome of the contest comes to symbolic expression at the end of the story: the sun rises, but Jacob is limping. The dark night of the soul has, to be sure, given way to the sunrise. But even so, no one who struggles with God walks away the same. In the fight that heals him, Jacob is wounded by God. He is left with a "thorn in [his] flesh," to borrow a term from the apostle Paul (2 Corinthians 12:7), as a reminder of his transformation and the all-sufficiency of God's grace. A true meeting with God is always a transforming meeting, even a "wounding" meeting. It must inevitably dislocate and displace all other loves in our lives—the love of a life of my own, a successful career, even a successful ministry. God wants us, not our untarnished performances and records. Few of us are able to surrender such without suffering, like Jacob, some dislocation in the process.

Jacob has faced his past. He can now meet his brother. The renegade is so moved by what has happened that he renames the place Peniel, meaning "the face of God." Beyond the blessing that Jacob sought so persistently, something greater has been given him: he has seen God face to face.

No one, not even Jacob, sees God with unimpaired vision, however. We shall not in this life solve all the problems of the universe or prove the existence of God. We shall not know why we were born into such-and-such circumstances or why things have turned out as they have. We must walk by faith, not by sight. The Christian

life is not a luxury cruise with full services. It is a sortie behind enemy lines, the pioneering of a new route through unknown territory,
a first ascent up a heretofore unclimbed wall. Scripture, prayer, and
the community of believers in the church have been given to us as a
map by which to travel. A reliable map they are—but like all maps,
this one requires knowledge, faith, and trust.

The climax of the story, however, is not the wrestling match
beside the river, important as it is, but the meeting with Esau. Immediately, we are told, Jacob looks up and sees his brother coming with his four hundred men. Which is more frightful: to fall
into the clutches of a just and holy God, or those of a wronged
brother? For Jacob there is little difference. His elaborate scheme of
sending servants, flocks, and family ahead of him in droves func-
tions like clockwork, but in the end it is unnecessary: "But Esau
ran to meet Jacob and embraced him; he threw his arms around
his neck and kissed him." What an astounding response from this
dreaded Esau! Neither Esau nor Jacob appears "in character" in
this meeting. Both have become something they have never been
before—enhanced, converted, redeemed. Jacob's premeditated
calculations, Esau's spontaneous forgiveness—the tension and
dread in the story are suddenly turned into hilarity. Instead of falling on Jacob in revenge, Esau embraces him in reconciliation. The
avenger becomes the reconciler; the wronged brother overcomes
the wrongdoer with mercy. Jacob has dreaded seeing Esau's face.
And yet in the face of Esau, Jacob sees something that he has seen
only at the Jabbok: "For to see your face," says Jacob, "is like seeing
the face of God."

We began this chapter by saying that most people want to
meet God. But where do we meet God? Jacob sees God where he
least expects to. He sees the face of God when "a man" accosts
him at a transition point in life and forces him to acknowledge
who he really is. It is a fearful experience, a battle against despair,
when God himself seems to join the howling onslaught of Jacob's
conscience and contend against him. Nevertheless, Jacob emerges
from the struggle aware that God's grace and persistence, rather
than his checkered past, are in control of his life. Painful though

the experience is, God shapes Jacob through it to become a fit partner for himself, an "Israel" instead of a "Jacob."

Not only in the inward journey, however, does Jacob see God. In the outward journey to meet a wronged brother, who falls upon Jacob not with vengeance but with compassion, Jacob also discovers the face of God. In both the onslaught at the Jabbok and the offensive of Esau, the Divine Intruder breaks into Jacob's life, and in both intrusions Jacob sees the same face—the face of God.

Do people today still see the face of God as Jacob did? Indeed they do, although some may not be fully aware of it. Think back to the story of Erich Honecker. The Honeckers were not aware of it, but they saw the face of God in a Lutheran pastor and his family who followed the commandment of Jesus Christ to love their enemies. But why did they not recognize God's face? The answer is clear from Jacob's story: until we tie up with God and allow his grace to subdue our sin and rebellion, we do not see God in people and circumstances around us.

Yes, God still meets unworthy sinners in surprising and unmistakable ways. And by his grace, some respond, as did Jacob. Not long ago I received a letter from a young woman who had taken a course from me on St. Augustine. Augustine's tumultuous experience of fleeing from the God he was trying to find mirrored her own life. "The heart may shut itself away," said Augustine, "but it cannot hide from your sight, O God. Man's heart may be hard, but it cannot resist the touch of your hand."[3] How descriptive of Jacob, how descriptive of the young woman. The young woman was later accosted by the same grace that had found Jacob and Augustine. "After years of dark, fruitless searching," she wrote, "my Father has captured my heart in ways I never dreamed possible. My nomadic journey ended with Him rushing out to meet me like the father of the prodigal son."

When Jesus himself told the story of the prodigal son he must have fashioned his most famous of parables on Jacob's meeting with Esau. A man had two sons, said Jesus. The younger son offended his father and older brother, much as Jacob had offended Isaac and Esau, by demanding a share of the family inheritance that was not rightly his. Once in hand, the inheritance was squandered on things unworthy of the father's character. As with Jacob, there came a day of reckoning when the son came up short. Like Jacob, the younger son came to himself and went back home to confess what he had done. Like Jacob, he expected to meet with inflexible justice, perhaps even revenge. He was mistaken. He met with grace . . . indeed, he was accosted by it! While he was a long way off, his father saw him and had compassion on him and "ran and embraced him around the neck and kissed him." These words describing the father's reconciliation with the prodigal son are the same words describing Esau's merciful meeting with Jacob. Like Jacob, when the son found compassion from the father, there he stood face to face with God.

QUESTIONS FOR DISCUSSION

1. Have you ever fought a spiritual battle that, at least initially, appeared to be a mundane matter?

2. What does Jacob hope to get from God in the wrestling match?

3. God would rather "wrestle" with you than let you go. Does this bring fear, freedom, or peace?

4. Jacob was transformed by God's question, "Who are you?" How would you answer?

5. What do we need to let go, and what do we need to face, in order to go forward with God?

3

Fear of Inadequacy

Now Moses was tending the flock of Jethro his father-in-law, the priest of Midian, and he led the flock to the far side of the desert and came to Horeb, the mountain of God. There the angel of the Lord appeared to him in flames of fire from within a bush. Moses saw that though the bush was on fire it did not burn up. So Moses thought, "I will go over and see this strange sight—why the bush does not burn up."

When the Lord saw that he had gone over to look, God called to him from within the bush, "Moses, Moses!"

And Moses said, "Here I am."

"Do not come any closer," God said. "Take off your sandals, for the place where you are standing is holy ground." Then he said, "I am the God of your father, the God of Abraham, the God of Isaac and the God of Jacob." At this, Moses hid his face, because he was afraid to look at God.

The Lord said, "I have indeed seen the misery of my people in Egypt. I have heard them crying out because of their slave drivers, and I am concerned about their suffering. So I have come down to rescue them from the hand of the Egyptians and to bring them up out of that land into a good and spacious land, a land flowing with milk and honey—the home of the Canaanites, Hittites, Amorites, Perizzites, Hivites and Jebusites. And now the cry of the Israelites has reached me, and I have seen the way the Egyptians are oppressing them. So now, go. I am sending you to Pharaoh to bring my people the Israelites out of Egypt."

But Moses said to God, "Who am I, that I should go to Pharaoh and bring the Israelites out of Egypt?"

And God said, "I will be with you. And this will be the sign to you that it is I who have sent you: When you have brought the people out of Egypt, you will worship God on this mountain."

Moses said to God, "Suppose I go to the Israelites and say to them, 'The God of your fathers has sent me to you,' and they ask me, 'What is his name?' Then what shall I tell them?"

God said to Moses, "I am who I am. This is what you are to say to the Israelites: 'I am has sent me to you.'"

God also said to Moses, "Say to the Israelites, 'The Lord, the God of your fathers—the God of Abraham, the God of Isaac and the God of Jacob—has sent me to you.' This is my name forever, the name by which I am to be remembered from generation to generation. . . .'"

Moses answered, "What if they do not believe me or listen to me and say, 'The Lord did not appear to you'?"

Then the Lord said to him, "What is that in your hand?"

"A staff," he replied.

The Lord said, "Throw it on the ground." Moses threw it on the ground and it became a snake, and he ran from it. Then the Lord said to him, "Reach out your hand and take it by the tail." So Moses reached out and took hold of the snake and it turned back into a staff in his hand. "This," said the Lord, "is so that they may believe that the Lord, the God of their fathers—the God of Abraham, the God of Isaac and the God of Jacob—has appeared to you. . . .'"

Moses said to the Lord, "O Lord, I have never been eloquent, neither in the past nor since you have spoken to your servant. I am slow of speech and tongue."

The LORD said to him, "Who gave man his mouth? Who makes him deaf or mute? Who gives him sight or makes him blind? Is it not I, the LORD? Now go, I will help you speak and will teach you what to say."

—Exodus 3:1-15; 4:1-5,10-12

MOSES HAD BEEN RAISED as a favored son of Egypt. True, he had been cast adrift in the Nile as an infant—but once he was discovered by Pharaoh's daughter and taken under her wing, his fortunes improved dramatically. He became heir to all the opulence and opportunity in Egypt. If his early years were any measure by which to judge, he might have expected a life of prestige and prosperity.

But somewhere, somehow, the life he might have expected passed him by. He had run afoul of Pharaoh and had had to flee Egypt for sanctuary in the desolate expanses of the Sinai. The desert expanses that shielded him also sealed him in a life of utter obscurity: "Now Moses was tending the flock of Jethro his father-in-law, the priest of Midian." In midlife he finds himself an undistinguished herdsman in the service of his father-in-law. Nothing more.

Moses drives his flocks across the forgotten wastes of Midian and comes to a place that already in his day was revered as a holy site: Horeb, the mountain of God. There, in the numbing normalcy of a shepherd's life, God appears to him in a very abnormal way. A bush catches fire. That is a strange occurrence, to be sure, but not wholly unusual in the searing heat of the Sinai, where pitch-filled shrubs occasionally burst into flame. What is strange is that the bush is not consumed by the fire, and this attracts Moses' attention. Within the rounded crags and bulbous-shaped mountains of Sinai, blistered from the sun by day and haunted by bone-chilling cold at night, comes something exceptional. It is fire, burning but not consuming. Fire of this sort announces the presence of God.

The burning bush is a theophany, an appearance of God in a natural phenomenon. The phenomenon was startling enough to attract Moses' attention, but once he turned to investigate, the burning bush played no further role. God evidently takes no delight in performing marvels to astound his creatures. An event even as remarkable as this has meaning only insofar as it leads to hearing the word of God.

A student of mine once related a story from his faith journey that illustrates this point. In his early college years, agnostic and unhappy, the student found God absent and faith unattainable. One day, as he awaited the arrival of his sister at an African bus stop, he heard that a bus coming from the vicinity from which he awaited his sister had been ambushed by guerrillas. News of the attack changed a tedious wait into a nail-biting uncertainty. Minutes became hours. His desperation momentarily shattered his agnosticism, and he prayed that if God would deliver his sister safely that he would believe in God and serve him for the rest of his life. Twenty minutes later a bus arrived and off stepped his sister, safe and sound. By the student's own admission, the remarkable thing about the incident was not the safe arrival of his sister, but the effect it had on his faith. "Once I saw my sister was unharmed," he confessed, "I forgot the promise I had made, and God was no more real to me than he had been before."

Extraordinary occurrences, even miracles like burning bushes or the safe arrival of loved ones, do not produce faith. Faith comes only from hearing the word of the living God that is addressed to us personally. As Moses approaches the bush, he encounters not an object, but a person; a something turns into a Someone.

"Moses, Moses," calls God. "Here am I," responds Moses. God identifies himself as the God of Moses' fathers, "the God of Abraham, the God of Isaac and the God of Jacob." The God who introduces himself to Moses is not a newcomer or a walk-on God. Moses may be tempted to think that everything begins with his experience or depends on him. Likewise, we may be tempted to think that our experience of the Christian faith is the sum total of the gospel, or that God's work stands or falls with our work. But that is not the case. Like us, Moses is simply one part—a very important part, to be sure, but still only one part—of a saving activity that extends into the distant past. God had been at work among the Hebrews long before Moses, and he had established a record of faithfulness to which he appeals in calling Moses. Moses' call finds meaning only because it fits into a larger plan and history of God's activity on behalf of Israel. This is as significant for us today as it was for Moses, for it means that God's call and promises are grounded in a history of faithfulness to people like us in the past.

But God has not appeared to rehearse the past. He launches into a series of declarations, the first of which is "I have indeed seen the misery of my people." The English translation cannot reproduce the force of the Hebrew, which twice repeats the word for "seeing." The gist is something like, "Have I ever seen the misery of my people!" God knows everything about the affliction of his people, all their oppression and suffering. A volley of transitive verbs follows: "I have heard them crying out because of their slave drivers . . . I am concerned about their suffering . . . I have come down to rescue them . . . and to bring them up out of that land." Those are muscular declarations. God is not a detached observer in the universe, deaf to the cries of hurting people and indifferent to the plight of suffering. God is passionately devoted to the motley band of Hebrew slaves to which Moses is related. Most people of the day—and perhaps of ours too—thought God was in the business of helping those who could help themselves, as the saying goes; of undergirding and abetting the powerful, prestigious, and prosperous. Surely, slaves fell outside his purview. But at the burning bush Moses learns differently. God's character is defined not by nouns but by verbs—the sinews and muscles of language—and that character is engaged on behalf of people who know hardship, pain, and cruelty, whose powers and hopes are exhausted and who stand on the brink of despair.

It is not Moses who draws God's attention to the troubles of his people. It is God who initiates the conversation and assures Moses, with the intensity of the fire in the bush, that he does not intend to stand idly by in the face of his people's plight. That thought, presumably, comforted and encouraged Moses. But the ensuing thought does not comfort him: God does not intend to act alone. God repeats his litany of concern about the oppression of the Israelites, and then abruptly sweeps Moses into the plot: "So now, go. I am sending you to Pharaoh to bring my people the Israelites out of Egypt."

This is a most disturbing thought. If Moses was not alarmed when he saw the burning bush, he is now. If God intends to act, let him act—but why must it include our involvement? Why God should enlist the services of a man like Moses is not entirely clear. Why would a decorated veteran select raw recruits to go with him into battle? For reasons that are not always apparent, God ordains to accomplish his purposes in the world with our involvement. This truth may cause us to marvel—or choke—but it is so. Neither does God assign us only to minor parts. Moses is not sent to reconnoiter the situation, to check it out, not even to give it his best shot. Moses is assigned the lead role: "Go, for I am sending you to Pharaoh!" And the most troubling aspect of the command, as the ensuing story shows, is that God has no intentions of altering the terms of the call.

None of us can know the exact course of events that God will set before us. Moses, however, knows enough about Egypt to realize that a face-off with Pharaoh is an impossible task. All thoughts of the plan, which seemed pleasing enough in their theoretical phase, are abandoned as quickly as a person abandons meditation in a garden when a thunderstorm breaks loose. Moses has no ear for further plans.

But he has a list of excuses why he cannot comply. His first excuse is, "Who am I, that I should go to Pharaoh?" It is curious that Moses is more terrified of standing before another human being than he is of standing before God Almighty. But he is, and the prospect gives him cramps. He asks the same question we ask when faced with the daunting, "Who am I?" In this particular situation, there is good reason for the question, for Pharaoh is the uncontested leader of a veritable superpower. Moses, expatriate-become-shepherd, is no match for Pharaoh. Further, there is the task of unraveling this knot of Hebrews from centuries of intermingling in Egypt. Who could possibly accomplish such a task? Yet it is this to which God calls Moses. God's call drives Moses inward in self-searching and self-doubt. His inner fears exceed even his external obstacles. The call of God cuts the nerve of his self-confidence, hurling him into profound introspection and doubt.

The apostle Paul must have echoed Moses' insecurities when he faced the obstreperous Corinthian Christians and described his situation as "harassed at every turn—troubles outside and fears within" (2 Corinthians 7:5).

A modern Moses of sorts, Dietrich Bonhoeffer left an immortal testimony to a similar struggle as he sought to bear witness to the meaning of life in a Nazi prison. In a searching poem entitled "Who Am I?" Bonhoeffer writes,

Who am I? They often tell me
I step from my cell
calmly and cheerfully and boldly,
as a manager from his estate.
Who am I? They often tell me
I speak with my guards
as freely and friendly and serenely,
as though it were mine to command.
Who am I? They also tell me
I bear the days of misfortune
with composure, smiling and confident,
as one who is accustomed to victory.
Am I really what others say of me?
Or am I only what I know of myself?
Restless, longing, sick, like a bird in a cage,
struggling for breath, as if someone were choking me,
hungering for colors, for flowers, for the songs of birds,
thirsting for kind words, for human companionship,
shaking with rage at both tyranny and the slightest offenses,
dizzy from waiting for great events,
faint with fear for friends far removed,
tired and empty from praying, thinking, doing,
utterly spent, and ready to say farewell to it all?
Who am I? The one or the other?
Am I one person today and another tomorrow?
Am I both at the same time? A hypocrite before others

and a despicable whining weakling before myself?
Perhaps what is in me is like a defeated army,
fleeing in disarray before a victory already won?
Who am I? This lonely question makes sport of me.
Whoever I am, Thou knowest O God, I am thine.[1]

Like Bonhoeffer—like most of us—Moses stands before the irrevocable call of God and asks, "Who am I?"

God's response is so simple as to appear utterly insignificant: "I will be with you." We wonder if Moses even heard it. If he did, it must have seemed like an empty platitude in the face of an avalanche of difficulties and uncertainties. Moses needs hard facts, not formalities.

When I was a young father, I promised my daughter Corrie, who was perhaps four years old at the time, that I would take her to play in the park one Saturday afternoon. Something came up that prevented me from keeping my promise, so I asked a friend of mine named John if he would take her instead. John later related to me that as they were walking the two blocks from our house to the park, Corrie began to get cold feet. Her pace slackened and she announced that she did not want to go to the park after all. John asked why, and she explained that there was a mean boy there named Ricky who frightened her. "How old is Ricky?" asked John. "He's old," said Corrie, "at least eight or nine!" John was in his twenties, stood about 6 feet 3 inches tall, and weighed at least 200 pounds. He was strong and athletic. "Don't worry," he told Corrie, "I'm with you." In John's mind that was all that needed saying; it covered any eventuality that might happen, including the mischief of an eight-year-old playground bully. To him, his assurances concluded the matter. But not for Corrie. Anyone over four feet tall looked more or less alike to her, and the difference between a preadolescent bully and a strapping bodyguard was much less apparent to her four-year-old eyes than it was in reality. In the end, John persuaded Corrie to go to the park, and true to his word he protected her from playground mischief—but not without a ton of encouragement and a mile of patience.

Is not this virtually the same conversation that Moses has with God? "I will be with you" is scarcely a hollow platitude. It carries the pledge of the presence of the Creator and Lord of the universe. But not in Moses' mind—or often in ours. Our problems loom large and menacing before us. It often seems a toss-up whether our adversities or God's promises will win the day. The key is for Moses—as it was for my daughter—to hear the promise with the authority of the one who promises rather than from personal insecurities. Until the assurance "I will be with you" carries with it the full force of divine sovereignty and love, we shall not know what it means to trust God.

Moses now turns from doubting self to doubting God, from psychology to theology: "Suppose I go to the Israelites and say to them, 'The God of your fathers has sent me to you,' and they ask me, 'What is his name?' Then what shall I tell them?" This is Moses' second excuse. He has moved beyond introspection, now putting hard questions to God: "Who are you, really?" We all think we know the answer to that question until God begins making demands of us. In fair weather, we talk of God as an eternal spirit, first cause, prime mover, ground of being, benevolent creator, all-knowing, all-wise, infinite, unchangeable. Perhaps we even believe these things—or think we do. But these are easy answers that cannot be tested. Such concepts make few demands—and promise minimal transformation—of those who hold them. No one ever does what Moses is asked to do on the basis of such answers. The great German preacher and theologian Helmut Thielicke once said, "Tell me how high and lofty God is for you, and I'll tell you how little he means to you."[2]

When God intrudes in our lives and begins making us uncomfortable, the stock clichés no longer suffice. We do what Moses does—we begin to follow up on God's references, so to speak. We run a credit check, and begin learning for ourselves exactly who this Intruder might be. Who is this God who disturbs my routine, who makes such demands and gives such promises? What is his name? Will he really be with me, be there for my every need, be faithful no matter what? Is God, in other words, engaged with my life? Does he have a word for me? Is he really the One who sees and hears and comes down and saves and redeems, or is God simply an idea—perhaps even a consoling idea—but an idea nevertheless? We wonder about the motive behind Moses' question. Did Moses inquire of God's name as a way of clarifying God's identity and establishing proper lines of authority? Or was his question a way of evading God's call, like a raccoon that jumps into a creek and runs upstream in order to shake the hounds from its scent? Perhaps his motives were mixed, just as ours often are. But God's answer is not mixed. For the first time in Israel's history God discloses his personal name, "I am who I am." After Moses' first excuse God assured him, "I will be with you." We now learn that was more than a promise. It was also God's name, "I am."

Until this point in Israelite history God has been known as *El* (Divinity), *Elohim* (God), *El-Elyon* (God Most High), *El-Olam* (God Everlasting), *Shaddai* (Almighty), *Abir* (Mighty One), *Adonai* (Lord), or *Pehad* (Fear). Calling the deity by such titles is like calling a person "homo sapiens" or "human being." Such titles are generic and impersonal, describing a "what," not a "who." But now, for the first time in history, from the flame beneath the mountain of God, God identifies himself not by a title but by his personal name, his unique identity. *Eh-yeh* is the Hebrew word. It is a strange and feeble-sounding name, is it not? Some hard consonants would make it more commanding, like Zeus, Thor, Re, or Shiva. But those are not the names Moses hears. He hears an unpretentious and baffling name, *Eh-yeh*.

We know that *Eh-yeh* is a form of the Hebrew verb "to be." For centuries scholars have debated its meaning. It can mean "I am who I am," or "I will be who I will be," or even "I will cause to be what is." One thing is clear from its present context: it is not just a designation for God, but it is also a statement of God's relationship to Israel. The great I am is a God of pathos, radically engaged with Israel: "I am with you."

Moses, like most of us, would like to have been given a name that would have proven God, an argument or fact that would have clinched God's existence. *Eh-yeh* does not do that. It does not identify God so much as God identifies the name. As Moses experiences more of God he will understand more of the name. God's character fills and gives meaning to this name, and about his character there is much less doubt. God gives his name in the context of the promise to rescue Israel from slavery in Egypt. It is surrounded by anticipation and hope. The way things are is not the way they always must be. God is bringing things into existence that do not yet exist. *Eh-yeh* is, after all, the same God who was with Abraham, Isaac, and Jacob. This God now promises to be with Moses and to continue in his experience the work he began in the patriarchs.

This brings Moses to his third excuse: "What if they do not believe me or listen to me and say, 'The Lord did not appear to you'?" This is an entirely predictable excuse. It is one we all employ—and often much sooner than Moses does. Moses is no longer thinking of himself or of God, but of the obstreperous Israelites. His thinking has moved from psychology to theology to interpersonal dynamics. He is impugning and blaming the Israelites.

Moses is shrewd enough to realize that his success in Egypt, whatever it may be, is dependent on others, and others are often fickle and unreliable. Sometimes they are even treacherous. Moses has no desire to hitch his cart to someone else's star, especially when the "someone" is the Israelites. "What chance of success do I have with people like this?" is the gist of his excuse. If Moses first doubted himself by asking, "Who am I?"—and then God by asking, "Who are you?"—he is now doubting those around him by asking, "Who are they?"

God asks Moses what is in his hand. A staff is in Moses' hand, a most common tool in a most common trade. "Throw it down on the ground," God commands. Moses does so, and to his dismay the staff becomes a snake. The Hebrew word means a large serpent, deadly and hissing; the word can also be used figuratively of an oppressor or enemy. Moses recoils in alarm. God commands Moses to pick it up . . . by the tail! Any kid who has hung around vacant lots or creek beds knows how to pick up a snake, and it is not by the tail. Moses surely knew that too, as did God. The command is a test

of Moses' faith. Moses has just complained of the Israelites' lack of
faith, but God is concerned with Moses' lack of faith. Moses may
be worried about the reliability of others, but God is thinking of
the reliability of Moses. The ultimate question in following God is
not whether others will be true, but whether we will be responsive
to the call God gives us—regardless of potential consequences.

In *The Chronicles of Narnia* by C. S. Lewis, Aslan, the majestic
Christlike lion, is sometimes asked what will happen in the future
or what Aslan will do in someone else's life. Aslan never answers
that question. "I tell no-one any story but his own," he always replies.[3] When Jesus met with the disciples after the Resurrection, he
was asked by Peter, "Lord, what about [John]?" Jesus answered that
whatever plans he has for John are not Peter's concern. "What is
that to you?" he responds. "You must follow me" (John 21:21-22).
And so it is with Moses: the issue at hand is not the faith of the
Hebrews but the faith of Moses.

God transforms Moses' staff into a vehicle of his presence
and power. All of us have tools of trade. For some, it is education, special skills, or training; for others, an interest in gardening,
music, building, or working with people; and for still others, it is a
vacation cabin, a gift of hospitality, or a passion for a cause. We all
have abilities and commitments that define who we are, some of
which we do well enough, as did Moses, to earn a living from. It is
these ordinary and common tools that God chooses to transform
for his purposes.

Most of us, I suspect, reserve the special occasions of life for
God, if we reserve any at all—the baptisms, weddings, anniver-
saries, promotions, and rare moments of genius and inspiration.
But special occasions and abilities are the exception, not the rule.
They come in increments of months, or even years, but we live
life day by day. Despite our occasional wishes to the contrary, life
is overwhelmingly routine. And it is its routineness that makes it
bearable. Holidays are special only because they are occasional. If
we lived all of life at the pitch of graduation week or our wedding
day, we would soon be withered and wasted. It is routine and normalcy that allow us to pay our bills and write letters and keep our

promises, to take walks and relax by the fire, to raise our children and enjoy our spouses and be with friends. It is in such activities that we learn faithfulness and forgiveness, constancy and character—the virtues that we value in others. It is in the everyday—in the study halls and commuter trains and board rooms and laundry rooms—that God is either Lord or nothing. God chooses the ordinary to become the manifestation of his presence.

"Who are they?" How many of us excuse our failures by pointing to the failures of others? I could have amounted to something, we say to ourselves, if only. . . . If only I had been raised in a different home or in some other place . . . had married a different person . . . had better teachers or coaches . . . had not been saddled with a particular temperament or illness . . . worked for better bosses . . . lived in a more stimulating environment. How easily we succumb to the idea that we are victims of more powerful people or inexorable circumstances.

The things that might have been are endless. Indeed, our résumés and vitas would read differently if we had different experiences and connections, but anyone who has compiled a résumé knows how little it actually discloses of self. The litany of if onlys might lead to different data, but would it make of us different persons? Most prisoners, I fear, discover that they are the same individuals outside as they were behind bars, just as most of us are no happier with our new toys than we were with our old ones.

Moses' third excuse is, in part at least, a projection of his own inadequacies onto the Hebrews. He points to their lack of belief as an excuse for his unwillingness to act. How typical of human nature to tailor our self-image and even our response to God to what we imagine others think of us. We feel victimized by the authorities or our bosses or spouses, and this becomes a justification for doing and being far less than we are capable of.

The gist of Moses' third excuse is, "I cannot do your will, God, because of the Israelites." In fairness to Moses, the Israelites were an undesirable lot. I doubt that any of us, given the choice, would throw our gear in their wagons. The burden of this people was real and overwhelming, and the Bible is utterly realistic about both

their inclinations and their effect on Moses. Moses' third excuse
seems imminently justified.

Moses does not have an easy decision. But to say there are
no easy answers is not to say there are no answers. There is at least
one answer, and that is to stop living within the confinements that
define others. It is one thing to empathize with the failed choices
and destructive values of others; it is quite another to allow them
to determine our own. God has given us sovereign charge of one
life, and that is our own. It is that for which we are ultimately held
accountable. To be human means to have at least some choices.
The only time that there are no more moves on the board is when
we are dead. Until then, God holds us, as he holds Moses, responsible for what we can and ought to do. More than that, he holds
us responsible, as he holds Moses, not to limit his sovereignty by
human failure and inadequacy—whether of ourselves or others.
God refuses to discuss "the Israelites" with Moses. He repeats the
command, "Go!"

The final excuse of Moses is less theoretical and more practical, indeed more desperate, than the first three. Moses senses that
he cannot outlast God. The Divine Intruder is closing the distance
on him. As the net tightens, Moses becomes more frantic. "O Lord,
I have never been eloquent, neither in the past nor since you have
spoken to your servant. . . . O Lord, please send someone else"
(Exodus 4:10,13). Moses is not a "man of words," but, according
to the Hebrew, "thick of tongue and heavy of mouth." He does not
have the ability to match words and ideas in order to move the
hearts and wills of his hearers. It is a glaring omission in his tran-
script, so to speak. Surely this would disqualify him for the task to
which God is calling him.

Centuries later a pioneer missionary from Tarsus admitted
to the sophisticated Corinthians that he too was ineloquent (2
Corinthians 10:10). But Paul responded to his deficiency differently than did Moses. Paul did not rule out his call on the basis
of his own inadequacies, but rested his case in God's power to
complete his calling. He recalls that he did not come to the Corinthians "with eloquence or superior wisdom. . . . I came to you

in weakness and fear, and with much trembling. My message and my preaching were not with wise and persuasive words, but with a demonstration of the Spirit's power, so that your faith might not rest on men's wisdom, but on God's power" (1 Corinthians 2:1-5). The apostle recognized that human abilities can be a trap, luring us to put ultimate trust in them rather than in their divine source. Ironically, both Paul and Moses are remembered as two of the most influential people in human history. Such is God's power in human weakness.

God makes no attempt to try to convince Moses that he is eloquent. So far as the record goes, God accepts Moses' self-assessment. But that does not change the call. God never changes the call, for the call is but the human side of the unchangeable purpose of God. Human inadequacy and weakness make obvious our need of God, and make us more open to God. The success of the call is not in our abilities, but our dependence on God.

A few years ago I received a telephone call asking if I would debate a vocal proponent of a controversial issue before a key church assembly. I was asked to present a scriptural argument for my position, which differed from my opponent's. My immediate response was to decline. The debate would be a turkey shoot for the other side, for neither my learning nor credentials matched those of my opponent. But there were no compelling reasons to decline. I felt I had to accept, which I reluctantly did.

As I prepared for the debate I was caught in a whirlpool of doubts. I envisioned a humiliating defeat before colleagues and acquaintances. I rued accepting the assignment, resentful that someone smarter and more knowledgeable had not been enlisted. I knew nothing of debate, I had never even been in a debate, and I felt I lacked the ego strength and quick thinking that debate demanded. I also knew from reputation that the particular assembly was slanted in favor of the other side. Why should I be a sacrificial lamb for their mistaken cause?

My soul was beset with all the fears and excuses of Moses. I doubted self, God, others, and my own abilities and calling. As I thrashed about in this mental morass, a new thought came to me.

It was not from a burning bush, but I believe it was from God. My job was not to prevail, achieve victory, or defeat an opponent. My assignment rather was to set forth the scriptural teaching on an important issue as intelligibly, forthrightly, fairly, and compassionately as I could. That was all. This was what I had been asked to do, and this I could do. This thought halted my downward spiral and sent me to the debate a much different person. I was less obsessed with self and more confident in the truth of Scripture. It was not "my position" but God's revealed word to which I was called to bear witness, the outcome of which I was willing to entrust to the Holy Spirit.

Something happened in the debate that I still do not fully understand. A toss of the coin allowed me to speak first. I was allowed twenty minutes, which I used to set forth the scriptural teaching as cogently as I could. My opponent then followed. Five or six minutes into his presentation he began to lose focus. He spoke louder, almost desperately, and suddenly slammed his fist on the podium in frustration, sending a sonic boom through the public address system. His argument had dissolved and he began repeating over and over that he was right. That debate was over!

The debate actualized the story of Moses in my own experience. I learned not to make light of Moses' excuses, but I also learned not to minimize or underestimate the power of God to breathe life into his word. Where our own inadequacies and deficiencies bear down on us inescapably, we often have to search for alternatives and substitutes. This can lead us to discover the greatest truth and power of all, the "I am who is with you."

The call of Moses began with God breaking into Israel's life when it was controlled and enslaved by Egypt. But God breaks into Israel's life by first breaking into the life of Moses, who, like Israel, is enslaved by his own fears of inadequacy. The excuses of Moses are more than his own personal excuses. They are also the excuses of greater Israel, of which Moses is a part, and by which he, knowingly or not, is influenced and determined. God overcomes Moses' excuses by his sovereign patience and purpose. God does not explain and defend his call; he declares it in sovereign authority.

God does not rebuke Moses; he dialogues with him, wears him out, wins him over. God does not rescind the call; he repeats it. Despite all Moses' objections and protests, God draws him into his saving purpose for Israel.

"Who am I?" "Who are you?" "Who are they?" "What can I do?" These are Moses' four excuses. How typically human. Somehow God accomplishes his will within them. The Divine Intruder has made an opponent into a partner; the heat of conflict has resulted in God and Moses alloyed in the divine will.

The greatest moment in Israel's history is about to begin: "Moses and Aaron went to Pharaoh and said, 'This is what the Lord, the God of Israel, says: "Let my people go" (Exodus 5:1).'"

QUESTIONS FOR DISCUSSION

1. Do you think Moses' excuses are genuine, or simply attempts to evade God's call?

2. Why does God's call usually come in ordinary rather than in extraordinary circumstances?

3. God's promise, "I will be with you," does not seem very convincing to Moses. What was he hoping for in the crisis?

4. What does your "if only"-list look like?

5. If you could ask Moses the one thing he learned, what do you think he would say?

4

Faith to Act

Again the Israelites did evil in the eyes of the Lord, and for seven years he gave them into the hands of the Midianites. Because the power of Midian was so oppressive, the Israelites prepared shelters for themselves in mountain clefts, caves and strongholds. Whenever the Israelites planted their crops, the Midianites, Amalekites and other eastern peoples invaded the country. They camped on the land and ruined the crops all the way to Gaza and did not spare a living thing for Israel, neither sheep nor cattle nor donkeys. They came up with their livestock and their tents like swarms of locusts. It was impossible to count the men and their camels; they invaded the land to ravage it. Midian so impoverished the Israelites that they cried out to the Lord for help.

When the Israelites cried to the Lord because of Midian, he sent them a prophet, who said, "This is what the Lord, the God of Israel, says: I brought you up out of Egypt, out of the land of slavery. I snatched you from the power of Egypt and from the hand of all your oppressors. I drove them from before you and gave you their land. I said to you, 'I am the Lord your God; do not worship the gods of the Amorites, in whose land you live.' But you have not listened to me."

The angel of the Lord came and sat down under the oak in Ophrah that belonged to Joash the Abiezrite, where his son Gideon was threshing wheat in a winepress to keep it from the Midianites. When the angel of the Lord appeared to Gideon, he said, "The Lord is with you, mighty warrior."

"But sir," Gideon replied, "if the Lord is with us, why has all this happened to us? Where are all his wonders that our fathers told us about when they said, 'Did not the Lord bring us up out of Egypt?' But now the Lord has abandoned us and put us into the hand of Midian."

The Lord turned to him and said, "Go in the strength you have and save Israel out of Midian's hand. Am I not sending you?"

"But Lord," Gideon asked, "how can I save Israel? My clan is the weakest in Manasseh, and I am the least in my family."

The Lord answered, "I will be with you, and you will strike down all the Midianites together."

Gideon replied, "If now I have found favor in your eyes, give me a sign that it is really you talking to me. Please do not go away until I come back and bring my offering and set it before you."

And the Lord said, "I will wait until you return."

Gideon went in, prepared a young goat, and from an ephah of flour he made bread without yeast. Putting the meat in a basket and its broth in a pot, he brought them out and offered them to him under the oak.

The angel of God said to him, "Take the meat and the unleavened bread, place them on this rock, and pour out the broth." And Gideon did so. With the tip of the staff that was in his hand, the angel of the Lord touched the meat and the unleavened bread. Fire flared from the rock, consuming the meat and the bread. And the angel of the Lord disappeared. When Gideon realized that it was the angel of the Lord, he exclaimed, "Ah, Sovereign Lord! I have seen the angel of the Lord face to face!"

But the Lord said to him, "Peace! Do not be afraid. You are not going to die."

So Gideon built an altar to the Lord there and called it The Lord is Peace. To this day it stands in Ophrah of the Abiezrites.

That same night the Lord said to him, "Take the second bull from your father's herd, the one seven years old.

Tear down your father's altar to Baal and cut down the Asherah pole beside it. Then build a proper kind of altar to the Lord your God on the top of this height. Using the wood of the Asherah pole that you cut down, offer the second bull as a burnt offering."

So Gideon took ten of his servants and did as the Lord told him. But because he was afraid of his family and the men of the town, he did it at night rather than in the daytime. . . .

Now all the Midianites, Amalekites and other eastern peoples joined forces and crossed over the Jordan and camped in the Valley of Jezreel. Then the Spirit of the Lord came upon Gideon, and he blew a trumpet, summoning the Abiezrites to follow him. He sent messengers throughout Manasseh, calling them to arms, and also into Asher, Zebulun and Naphtali, so that they too went up to meet them.

Gideon said to God, "If you will save Israel by my hand as you have promised—look, I will place a wool fleece on the threshing floor. If there is dew only on the fleece and all the ground is dry, then I will know that you will save Israel by my hand, as you said." And that is what happened. Gideon rose early the next day; he squeezed the fleece and wrung out the dew—a bowlful of water.

Then Gideon said to God, "Do not be angry with me. Let me make just one more request. Allow me one more test with the fleece. This time make the fleece dry and the ground covered with dew." That night God did so. Only the fleece was dry; all the ground was covered with dew.

Early in the morning, Jerub-Baal (that is, Gideon) and all his men camped at the spring of Harod. The camp of Midian was north of them in the valley near the hill of Moreh. The Lord said to Gideon, "You have too many men for me to deliver Midian into their hands. In order that Israel may not boast against me that her own strength has saved her, announce now to the people, 'Anyone who trembles with fear may turn back and leave Mount Gilead.'" So twenty-two thousand men left, while ten thousand remained.

But the Lord said to Gideon, "There are still too many men. Take them down to the water, and I will sift them for you there. If I say, 'This one shall go with you,' he shall go; but if I say, 'This one shall not go with you,' he shall not go."

So Gideon took the men down to the water. There the Lord told him, "Separate those who lap the water with their tongues like a dog from those who kneel down to drink." Three hundred men lapped with their hands to their mouths. All the rest got down on their knees to drink.

The Lord said to Gideon, "With the three hundred men that lapped I will save you and give the Midianites into your hands. Let all the other men go, each to his own place." So Gideon sent the rest of the Israelites to their tents but kept the three hundred, who took over the provisions and trumpets of the others. . . .

Gideon returned to the camp of Israel and called out, "Get up! The Lord has given the Midianite camp into your hands." Dividing the three hundred men into three companies, he placed trumpets and empty jars in the hands of all of them, with torches inside.

"Watch me," he told them. "Follow my lead. When I get to the edge of the camp, do exactly as I do. When I and all who are with me blow our trumpets, then from all around the camp blow yours and shout, 'For the Lord and for Gideon.'"

Gideon and the hundred men with him reached the edge of the camp at the beginning of the middle watch, just after they had changed the guard. They blew their trumpets and broke the jars that were in their hands. The three companies blew the trumpets and smashed the jars. Grasping the torches in their left hands and holding in their right hands the trumpets they were to blow, they shouted, "A sword for the Lord and for Gideon!" While each man held his position around the camp, all the Midianites ran, crying out as they fled.

When the three hundred trumpets sounded, the Lord caused the men throughout the camp to turn on each other with their swords. The army fled.

—Judges 6:1-27,33-40; 7:1-8,15-22

Someone traversing the central hill country of Palestine about 1100 b.c. might have been baffled by the sight of a man threshing grain in a winepress. But then again, he probably would not have noticed him at all, for the man did not want to be seen.

The man's name was Gideon, and he was a member of a one-man underground. We know that because of his odd behavior. Wheat should be threshed in open fields or exposed places so that the wind can blow the chaff away when the wheat is thrown into the air, allowing the grain to fall to the ground. Pressing wine was an inside job for storerooms or dens or caves. No one would thresh wheat in the cramped and unventilated quarters of a winepress unless he did not want people to know what he was doing.

And that explains Gideon's clandestine industry. Like any number of desperate Israelites, Gideon is trying to eke out a living under the thumb of the Midianites, camel-riding raiders east of the Gulf of Aqaba far to the south. With their Bedouin allies—Amalek and other eastern desert tribes—the Midianites have swept into Israel thick as a locust plague. They have surrounded Israel like a scimitar, from the hill country in the north to Gaza down south, wasting her crops and rustling and hamstringing her livestock. Midian has a vise grip on Israel's food supply, forcing the Israelites to become refugees in their own land by fleeing into the caves and dens that pockmark the central hill country. The vise grip has continued for seven years, and Israel is in a crisis; hence, the threshing of grain in a winepress to keep it from falling into the hands of the enemy.

The crisis, unfortunately, is nothing new, but simply another episode in a pattern of sorry episodes that befell Israel from about 1200 to 1000 b.c. This pattern is painfully clear in the book of Judges, which recounts our story. First, God delivers Israel from a crisis, and deliverance is followed by a season of prosperity. Prosperity leads not to gratitude and obedience, however, but to complacency, and complacency to forgetfulness, and forgetfulness to sin. In anger, God hands Israel over to its enemies. From the pain of oppression Israel repents and cries out for help. God hears the cry and sends a helper, a "judge" according to the Hebrew—or as we would say today, a "freedom fighter." Victory ushers in a period of prosperity, and the pattern repeats itself.

Israel has again forgotten God, relapsed into disobedience, and fallen under the judgment of God. Enter Midian and their ilk. In the original Hebrew, "Israel has been laid very low before the Midianites" (Judges 6:6).

"Laid very low." How often that condition is fertile ground for a new and unforeseen harvest—even in a winepress. No one, of course, likes being laid low, and when we are laid low our usual sense is that we have been abandoned. But at this point our sense is wrong. That is clear from the story of Gideon, and from the Bible as a whole: "Though the Lord is on high, he looks upon the lowly" (Psalm 138:6). The Lord not only looks, he enters—whether invited or not.

The theology department in which I taught assigns a series of final papers for theology majors in their senior year. One of them is a spiritual autobiography. As I read through the twenty-five or so spiritual autobiographies that students submit each spring, I am struck by the hardships, even tragedies, that many of our students have known . . . divorce, death, abuse and abandonment, illness, siblings with birth defects, financial collapse, automobile accidents, shootings. I feel humbled and chastened by their stories, but I am also amazed by a profound irony that often results from such adversities. Many students attest that precisely in such evils God was present in ways they had not known before and could never have imagined, breaking through, seizing and sustaining them, and drawing them to new or more vital faith.

An interesting theory of personal suffering was put forth by Origen, the third-century church father. Origen believed that in the eyes of God each of us has been allotted a particular constitution as our appropriate sparring partner. Each person's flesh and blood is peculiar to that person, taught Origen, and has been expressly calibrated by God to challenge the potential in each individual to stretch beyond himself or herself. The gentle precision of God's mercy ensures that our constitutions are adjusted to the peculiar needs of our souls down to the finest details. In the eyes of God, the temptations of one person are as different from those of another as are their fingerprints or handwriting. "You have coals of fire," said Origen. "You will sit upon them, and they will be of help to you."[1]

The coals that Origen speaks of do not consume, they help. They will even help Gideon, although he has a hard time believing it. But in order to help, God must address a need that Gideon does not know he has. "When the Israelites cried to the Lord because of Midian, he sent them a prophet, who said, 'This is what the Lord, the God of Israel, says: I brought you up out of Egypt, out of the land of slavery. I snatched you from the power of Egypt and from the hand of all your oppressors. I drove them from before you and gave you their land.'" What a perplexing word this is. It is, to be sure, reassuring to know that God hears and speaks to Israel, but it is not the word Israel hopes to hear. Israel needs deliverance, not a history lesson. Israel, we may be certain, knew the story of the Exodus and was thankful for deliverance from Egypt, much as we, perhaps, are thankful for "God's bounty" at Thanksgiving. But at the same time, this particular word must have seemed formulaic and hollow, like the kinds of things officials and authorities say when trying to put the best face on a catastrophe. Israel sends an emergency SOS; God replies with a word to remember. Israel is urgent and desperate; God indulges in an exercise of memory. The divine response scarcely seems appropriate to the exigencies at hand.

God often answers in surprising, even confounding, ways. In this particular case, the problem is not primarily the Midianites, although it appears so to Israel. The problem is Israel's repeated forgetfulness of God. Before Israel can hope, Israel must remember. In order to hear God's word in the present, Israel must remember his saving acts and faithfulness in the past.

In the midst of crisis, God does something quite characteristic of God: he calls a single individual to make a difference, which brings us back to Gideon in the winepress. An angel of the Lord appears under an oak tree to Gideon. We cannot say for sure, but there may be divine irony in this particular act. The Hebrew word for "oak" refers more specifically to terebinth or pistachio trees, which were often sites for the worship of fertility gods and goddesses. We do not know that Gideon observed such carnal rites, but we learn shortly after this episode that on the property of his father there is an altar to Baal, the Amorite storm god, and a wooden pole erected to Asherah, the mother goddess of Ugarit. Baal and Asherah were powerful fertility deities of the Canaanites whose conjugal rites were celebrated under terebinths. If this particular terebinth was one of the "spreading leafy trees" so often castigated by the prophets, then the angel's placement under the tree is a lesson with a diamond point to it: from now on Gideon is to look to God, not to pagan rituals.

The angel's dialogue with Gideon, like God's earlier speech to Israel, seems curiously out of step with Gideon's world. As always, the first word begins with God: "The Lord is with you, mighty warrior." That statement surely left Gideon staring at his feet. The Hebrew term here translated "mighty warrior" can also be translated "mighty man of valor," meaning a freeman as opposed to a slave, a man of substance and status who could serve in the army—or provide a substitute for himself if he chose not to. But in Gideon's circumstances, "man of valor" must have seemed either humorous exaggeration or outright sarcasm! Gideon has been living a double life: servile in public, conspiring in private. He has been working on the sly, slinking in the shadows. How can God dignify Gideon's furtive behavior as valorous and brave?

How amazing that the angel does not upbraid, condemn, and shame Gideon, however appropriate that might be. A friend of mine recently underwent three heart surgeries in less than one year. After two of the surgeries his vital signs fell precipitously and the medical teams abandoned hopes of his recovery. But survive he did, and the staff dubbed him "Lazarus." My friend refers to those experiences as "three trips down 'the valley of the shadow of death.'" He continues, "God intruded himself into my experience in a way he never had before—or had never been allowed to. One of the most marvelous aspects of that experience is that except for some struggle immediately after that first surgery, the Lord never confronted me with any of my past sins and failures, wrong turns, or foolish decisions. Rather, he seems to have assured me that 'It is well with my soul.'" Perhaps Gideon's conscience convicts him likewise. But the conscience is not God, nor is its voice the word of God: "If our heart condemns us, God is greater than our heart, and knows all things" (1 John 3:20, NKJV). God sees in Gideon something that Gideon may not see in himself. God sees in Gideon not only what he is, but what he will become by God's transforming call—and he addresses him accordingly. At the moment Gideon is only a small operator, but God will make him a mighty warrior.

God is in the business of transforming what is into what might be. Censure does not achieve that transformation, but solidarity and affirmation do. That is why God comes to us in our deepest troughs and needs with his forgiving and saving presence rather than with condemning judgment. At the point where we are most vulnerable and alone, God says, "I am with you."

When I was thirty-two I was diagnosed with melanoma. The cancer was a stage four, which indicated it was advanced and fast-spreading. As I was being wheeled to the operating room I experienced a loneliness greater than anything I had ever known. In that moment I discovered that the physical presence of my wife and parents made all the difference in the world. The love and presence of my family were a veritable incarnation of God's presence. I learned something from that experience that the Bible teaches us in the stories of Moses and Gideon and many others—that crises in life are not always solved by answers. Would it, after all, lessen the pain of a person dying of cancer or of parents at the loss of a child to know why such tragedies befell them? When there are no answers, life is sustained and made bearable by companionship. "I am with you," says God to Gideon.

But like Moses, Gideon finds that promise difficult to believe. Even if he believes it, he finds it of doubtful significance: "'But sir,' Gideon replied, 'if the Lord is with us, why has all this happened to us? Where are all his wonders that our fathers told us about when they said, "Did not the Lord bring us up out of Egypt?" But now the Lord has abandoned us and put us into the hand of Midian.'"

Pain clears the mind of illusions. Hardships and adversities pare away the extraneous in life and make all of us a good deal more practical. The grinding realities of life under Midianite occupation have had this effect on Gideon. He is in no mood for God-talk and spiritual clichés. A woman once wrote to me after she had lost her job, "And don't try smoothing things over by saying, 'When God closes one door he opens another.'" Gideon would have said "Amen" to that. His retort is clear, blunt, passionate: "If the Lord is with us, why has all this happened to us?" It reminds me of the prayer to God attributed to Teresa of Avila: "No wonder You have so few friends when You treat the ones You have so badly." If God was with our forebears and did marvelous things, why when he claims to be with us have such miseries befallen us?

It is easy to talk this way, and perhaps most of us do when life runs amok. But there is a flaw in the reasoning—the same flaw that appears in the reasoning of Job's friends. They argue—they argue wrongly—that good things happen to good people and bad things to bad people. Job understands a deeper, if more perplexing, reality: There is not always a predictable correlation between our character and our experiences. There is a mysterious sense in which suffering and hardship are necessary for our spiritual maturity. Moreover, the struggle between God's promises and the pain of human existence is more often than not the crucible of faith.

Listen to these words from another questioner of God.

> The school of life has some difficult classes. But it is in these classes that one learns the most. My most difficult class came in a prison cell of four walls, six steps long and two wide, and a door that could only be opened from the outside. Outside there was electrified barbed wire and a gate guarded by machine guns.[2]

This was the classroom of Corrie ten Boom in a Nazi concentration camp. Or ponder Aleksandr Solzhenitsyn's statement that he was thankful for the Gulag. Anyone familiar with the Stalinist concentration camp system will find that statement shocking,

perhaps unbelievable. It was, however, in the Gulag that Solzhenitsyn claims to have learned the two most important lessons of life:
what is in the heart of man, and the meaning of the gospel.

God does not answer all Gideon's questions. Rather, God
commands Gideon to act in the strength or might God has given
him. "The Lord turned to [Gideon] and said, 'Go in the strength
you have and save Israel out of Midian's hand. Am I not sending
you?'" The record of God's dealing with his people is not up for
question. The word of God comes to Gideon not as a theological
discussion or counseling session. There is no grievance committee in heaven. God's word comes as a command, a summons to
action—"Go in the strength you have."

It must seem to Gideon that he has no strength; he might have
thought, "Act on what?" His days consist in lurking among trifling
options in the face of swift and ironclad efficiency from Midian.
"But Lord," Gideon asked, "how can I save Israel? My clan is the
weakest in Manasseh, and I am the least in my family." Gideon's
rebuttal, like so many, is founded in a good deal of truth. Take his
tribe, Manasseh, for example. Manasseh had to share its allotment
of land with the tribe of Ephraim. Ephraim and Manasseh were
commonly called "half-tribes"—and at the moment Gideon is particularly cognizant of the "half." Numerically speaking, Manasseh
was the smallest tribe in Israel, even smaller than tiny Benjamin
(Numbers 2). Manasseh was a tribe with an "attitude," perhaps because of its smallness. Back in the days of the Exodus, five women
from Manasseh approached Moses and challenged the custom that
women could not inherit property. Zelophehad their father, had
had no sons to whom to bequeath his property and his daughters
did not want to see their father's inheritance vanish—and their
livelihood with it. It was a cheeky request on their part, but they
prevailed and ushered in a new era of property rights.

Gideon is no less importunate than the earlier matriarchs of
Manasseh. Think about it: God addresses Gideon as "mighty warrior" at the point where Gideon laments being least in the family of
the weakest clan of the smallest tribe of Israel. That spells a problem
when your enemies are camel-riding raiders thick as a locust plague.

Gideon has no status, rank, title, education, or prestige that we know of; none of the things, in other words, that count for something in the world. Gideon assumes his deficits are serious enough to scuttle the call, and I suspect that if we were reading his résumé we might agree. But God, as we have seen before, grounds his election of us in something other than "the facts." God speaks in the imperative— Go! Do! Say! Be! Gideon responds in the interrogative—What? How? Why? Me? In the fray of command and counterquestion, in the struggle with promise and disbelief, faith is born.

God, however, does not linger over Gideon's objections and inferiorities. The word can't is not in the divine vocabulary. Without argument, God holds to the promise: "I will be with you, and you will strike down all the Midianites together." To this, Gideon replies, "If now I have found favor in your eyes, give me a sign that it is really you talking to me. Please do not go away until I come back and bring my offering and set it before you." The word of God is beginning to work on Gideon. He can no longer dismiss it as a momentary mirage, but that does not mean he fully accepts it either. In fact, once Gideon accepts the reality of God's intervention in his life, the battle begins in earnest. He wants something empirical, something tangible and verifiable to confirm to himself and others that the risk he is being asked to take is worth it. This is the acid test of faith—not whether it is intellectually satisfying, but whether it is something on which we are willing to stake our existence, to act.

God is not put off by Gideon's tests. Indeed, God appears to welcome them because they are a first step in acting on God's word: "I will wait until you return," he says. Gideon now embarks on a series of proofs—one concerning his offering, the more famous concerning a woolen fleece. These are things that Gideon must do if he is to trust in God. Let this dispel any notion that earlier ages found faith easier than ours does. What naïveté to suppose that faith has ever been easy, the "natural response" of an individual.

Mainstream Christianity, in particular, often disdains the search for signs as something crass and unworthy of genuine belief. "Informed faith," it would have us believe, needs no such props and proofs. But I wonder if such enlightened religion is not often a cloak for unbelief. Are we above what God allows, even encourages? There was a famous king in the Old Testament who said he would not put God to the test, but his protest was only a pious charade. In reality, he was too afraid to ask for a sign (Isaiah 7). It takes faith to seek a sign of God's will.

A bolder step is now required of Gideon: "That same night the Lord said to him, '. . . Tear down your father's altar to Baal and cut down the Asherah pole beside it. Then build a proper kind of altar to the Lord your God on the top of this height. . . .' So Gideon took ten of his servants and did as the Lord told him. But because he was afraid of his family and the men of the town, he did it at night rather than in the daytime." Some of God's commands produce outright fear in us, as this one did in Gideon. God orders Gideon to tear down an altar to false gods and build an altar to the true God in its place. False gods and close friends often go together, as they do in Gideon's case. He is afraid of what the neighbors might think; he wants to maintain his reputation as well as his faith. We may be inclined to denigrate Gideon for his fears. True faith, we say, does not act in the dark but in broad daylight. Perhaps so. But who has true faith? God seems willing to accept less than true faith, even faith the size of a mustard seed, or faith mixed with superstition, or in this case, faith trembling with fear. What act of faith, however genuine, is not compromised or qualified or hedged by similar motives on our part? It is surely a false idealism to assert that only pure faith pleases God. God is not so proud as that. What does please God is when faith, however weak, prevails over cowardice or superstition or fear. That happens in Gideon's case. He tears down the bogus altar and builds a proper one, as God commands.

Put yourself in a position I have been in many times as a mountaineer. You are perched atop a towering summit, about to begin a rappel. A great chasm yawns beneath your feet. Your head swims with vertigo. On a purely intellectual level you know that the rappel is safe: the piton, or anchor, to which the rope is attached is secure as a bunker; the double strands of nylon rope in your hands will hold several tons of weight; the carabiner mechanism through which you run the rope to create friction and slow your fall is solid titanium and foolproof. You follow the rope, gently undulating in the breeze, to make sure it reaches to the ground. Everything is assured . . . except the act itself. You have to do the one thing that every fiber of your being resists: you must back off the cliff, slowly release your white-knuckled grip on the rope, and entrust your full weight to the rope.

I have rappelled many times in my life, and I have introduced many people to rappelling. No matter how often I rappel, I am never without fear, and I do not believe I have ever seen anyone else rappel without fear. When you understand rappelling, however, you do not expect to be without fear. The conflict of emotions raging within is simply part of the art. Fear, intense as it is, ceases to be the deciding factor. The rappel hinges entirely on the act, the moment of entrusting yourself to what you know to be true in spite of the protest of your senses.

Likewise with faith, we must act on what we know to be true, despite our fears. Gideon's fear is thus not the last word. It is indeed the penultimate word, but in the end he acts. God has not answered all his questions or eased all his fears. Like every rappeller I know, Gideon is not free from doubts, fears, protests, or cowardice, but he does the one thing he must do: he subordinates them to his greater trust in God. God succeeds in convincing Gideon to act on what he knows, and when he does, God delivers Israel through him.

I am grateful to have counted among my personal friends Corrie ten Boom, worker in the Dutch underground in World War II, survivor of a Nazi concentration camp, and itinerant evangelist. My wife and I once spent a week with Corrie in her home in Baarn, Holland. As we observed Corrie's pure and joyful trust in Jesus, we asked her, "What do we need to know to have faith like yours?" Her reply, vintage Corrie ten Boom for its simplicity, was, "You do not need to know anything more. You must live by what you already know!"

That simple advice captures Gideon's experience. He must remember what he knows, and he must act on what he believes.

Gideon's final response to God must be the final response of each of us: to translate trust into action. The anxious warrior must reduce his staff from thirty-two thousand to ten thousand, and then to a skeletal three hundred. This is to make Gideon poignantly aware that the victory belongs to God, not to his own strength. Jesus also sent out the twelve disciples with instructions to take only a staff and no provisions (Mark 6:7-11). He too was forcing them to go in faith, not in the number of their provisions. Jesus knew that the disciples would be believable only if they went in want, not in strength and full supply. Faith is faith not where it looks to safety and success, but where it braves risks in the name of obedience to Jesus Christ.

The great theologian Karl Barth reminded us that we have value in the church of Christ only insofar as we are weak. The weak know their need of God; they are not too proud to receive God through others, or to be used by God for others. The strong do not need others—they have nothing to learn.[3] They are, as Mother Teresa said of the rich, actually poorer and lonelier: "The more you have, the more you are occupied, the less you give." She continued, "[The rich] are never satisfied. . . . They always need something more. . . . I find that poverty hard to remove. The hunger for love is much more difficult to remove than the hunger for bread."[4]

The great irony of discipleship is that God must first make us weak in order to use us. He must, as Gideon's story reminds us, bring us low. This is God's program not simply for great acts of faith, but for every act of faith, even the smallest. So it was with Gideon. The Divine Intruder infiltrates Gideon's private undercover operation and transforms him from a petty menace to a national liberator, from a termite to a terminator. The Lord outlasts his laments of abandonment and inadequacy; he grants his requests for signs and overcomes his fears of what others think; and finally, he strengthens his resolve to act. God's intrusion in Gideon's life pulls him out of mothballs to become a warrior—it moves him from the sidelines to the line of scrimmage, from someone rendered immobile by the odds against him to a partner of God in overcoming those odds. Gideon is finally enabled to commit his cause to

God's expressed will, "For the Lord and for Gideon!" Gideon goes in weakness and want, but in so doing he goes in the might of the Lord of hosts, who "caused the men throughout the camp [of Midian] to turn on each other with their swords."

QUESTIONS FOR DISCUSSION

1. Why do we often find God or experience his presence most certainly when we are "laid low"?

2. In the Old Testament remembering God's faithfulness is the first and most important act of faith. Why might this be so?

3. God said to Moses, "I am with you," and to Gideon, "Am I not sending you?" Discuss the similar pattern in which both Moses and Gideon respond to God's promise.

4. Do you agree that faith is like rappelling—acting on something you know to be true but are afraid to trust?

5. What is the relationship between seeking a sign from God and acting in faith?

5

Grieved by Grace

The word of the Lord came to Jonah son of Amittai: "Go to the great city of Nineveh and preach against it, because its wickedness has come up before me."

But Jonah ran away from the LORD and headed for Tarshish. He went down to Joppa, where he found a ship bound for that port. After paying the fare, he went aboard and sailed for Tarshish to flee from the LORD.

Then the LORD sent a great wind on the sea, and such a violent storm arose that the ship threatened to break up. All the sailors were afraid and each cried out to his own god. And they threw the cargo into the sea to lighten the ship.

But Jonah had gone below deck, where he lay down and fell into a deep sleep. The captain went to him and said, "How can you sleep? Get up and call on your god! Maybe he will take notice of us, and we will not perish."

Then the sailors said to each other, "Come, let us cast lots to find out who is responsible for this calamity." They cast lots and the lot fell on Jonah.

So they asked him, "Tell us, who is responsible for making all this trouble for us? What do you do? Where do you come from? What is your country? From what people are you?"

He answered, "I am a Hebrew and I worship the LORD, the God of heaven, who made the sea and the land."

This terrified them and they asked, "What have you done?" (They knew he was running away from the LORD, because he had already told them so.)

The sea was getting rougher and rougher. So they asked him, "What should we do to you to make the sea calm down for us?"

"Pick me up and throw me into the sea," he replied, "and it will become calm. I know that it is my fault that this great storm has come upon you."

Instead, the men did their best to row back to land. But they could not, for the sea grew even wilder than before. Then they cried to the LORD, "O LORD, please do not let us die for taking this man's life. Do not hold us accountable for killing an innocent man, for you, O LORD, have done as you pleased." Then they took Jonah and threw him overboard, and the raging sea grew calm. At this the men greatly feared the LORD, and they offered a sacrifice to the LORD and made vows to him.

But the LORD provided a great fish to swallow Jonah, and Jonah was inside the fish three days and three nights. . . .

And the LORD commanded the fish, and it vomited Jonah onto dry land.

Then the word of the LORD came to Jonah a second time: "Go to the great city of Nineveh and proclaim to it the message I give you."

Jonah obeyed the word of the LORD and went to Nineveh. Now Nineveh was a very important city—a visit required three days. On the first day, Jonah started into the city. He proclaimed: "Forty more days and Nineveh will be overturned." The Ninevites believed God. They declared a fast, and all of them, from the greatest to the least, put on sackcloth.

When the news reached the king of Nineveh, he rose from his throne, took off his royal robes, covered himself with sackcloth and sat down in the dust. Then he issued a proclamation in Nineveh:

"By the decree of the king and his nobles:

Do not let any man or beast, herd or flock, taste anything; do not let them eat or drink. But let man and beast be covered with sackcloth. Let everyone call urgently on God. Let them give up their evil ways and their violence.

Who knows? God may yet relent and with compassion turn from his fierce anger so that we will not perish."

When God saw what they did and how they turned from their evil ways, he had compassion and did not bring upon them the destruction he had threatened. But Jonah was greatly displeased and became angry. He prayed to the LORD, "O LORD, is this not what I said when I was still at home? That is why I was so quick to flee to Tarshish. I knew that you are a gracious and compassionate God, slow to anger and abounding in love, a God who relents from sending calamity. Now, O LORD, take away my life, for it is better for me to die than to live."

But the LORD replied, "Have you any right to be angry?"

Jonah went out and sat down at a place east of the city. There he made himself a shelter, sat in its shade and waited to see what would happen to the city. Then the LORD God provided a vine and made it grow up over Jonah to give shade for his head to ease his discomfort, and Jonah was very happy about the vine. But at dawn the next day God provided a worm, which chewed the vine so that it withered. When the sun rose, God provided a scorching east wind, and the sun blazed on Jonah's head so that he grew faint. He wanted to die, and said, "It would be better for me to die than to live."

But God said to Jonah, "Do you have a right to be angry about the vine?"

"I do," he said. "I am angry enough to die."

But the LORD said, "You have been concerned about this vine, though you did not tend it or make it grow. It sprang up overnight and died overnight. But Nineveh has more than a hundred and twenty thousand people who cannot tell their right hand from their left, and many cattle as well. Should I not be concerned about that great city?"

—Jonah 1:1-17; 2:10–4:11

Gon's INTRUSION INTO OUR lives usually occurs in the face of contrary intentions on our part, and often outright resistance. Of no character is that truer than of Jonah. C. S. Lewis recounted his own reluctant pilgrimage to faith: from cocky atheism to agnosticism, then to uneasy theism, and finally to tremulous faith in Jesus Christ as the Son of God. He confessed that he was surely "the most dejected and reluctant convert in all England."[1] We may accept the truth of Lewis's word, but only because Jonah had never visited England.

Most of the stories in The Divine Intruder follow a certain pattern. God approaches a particular individual in the midst of routine existence—a shepherd tending sheep, a young woman planning to get married, an old man and his wife regretting that with advancing years their dreams have passed them by, a church leader lying low from fear of persecution. Into the midst of the ordinary comes something out of the ordinary, a concrete command of God. The believer's first response, predictably, is one of awe, often followed by guarded interest—until the magnitude of the task becomes apparent. Then, like a whale hit with a harpoon, the believer begins to fight. Excuses, protests, laments, pleas—all erupt from the volcano of the fully awakened soul, a soul that, if only for an instant, has perceived the awesome divide between God and itself. In contrast to the stormy human partner, God holds the rudder to a steady course, neither assailing in wrath nor recoiling in offense, repeating the command again and again until the wearied soul collapses into the arms of a holy love that it has long sought but feared to trust.

That is the normal pattern. Jonah, however, is the proverbial exception to the rule. Resistance—and this is no less true of resistance to God—can occur only when there is some sort of relationship. It is like the sail of a ship or an airplane wing, which work only in the face of opposition from the wind. But Jonah is one of those rare souls who will have none of it. There will be no relationship, no conversation from him. Jonah never speaks to God until the end of the story, and then only in anger. Abraham, Moses, and Gideon may dialogue with God, and Jacob may even contend with God, but not Jonah. Jonah short-circuits the whole process; when God speaks, he takes to his heels: "The word of the Lord came to Jonah son of Amittai: 'Go to the great city of Nineveh and preach against it, because its wickedness has come up before me.' But Jonah ran away from the Lord."

We must tell Jonah's side of the story, however, lest we think him apathetic or cowardly. He was neither. His noncompliance was perfectly understandable. Indeed, it was demanded by attitudes of the day, perhaps even by the dictates of morality. Two factors complicate Jonah's encounter with God that are absent from other encounters in this book. The first is that Jonah is the only prophet in the Old Testament called to preach to a nation other than Israel. In the shrinking global village and multicultural mentality of the twenty-first century, the call to go international may not seem very unusual. Indeed, it might seem to elevate Jonah's call, because a universal God is surely greater than a local and ethnic God. But not in Jonah's mind. The Hebrews had received a covenant with God that made them unique among the nations. By Jonah's day the uniqueness of God's "peculiar people," to quote the Hebrew (Exodus 19:5), was understood to imply strict separation from other nations. The separation of Jews from Gentiles led to a second factor in Jonah's thinking: he believed—and with some justification—that other nations were out to annihilate Israel. If you recall the determination of European Jews after World War II never to undergo a Holocaust again, you will have some idea how Jonah felt.

This second point requires a bit more elaboration. If not every people was out to destroy Israel, the particular city to which Jonah is directed certainly was. And it had ample means to do so. Nineveh was the capital of Assyria, a nation that in its day set a standard of dread and terror. The modern historian is hard put to find any virtues in Assyrian culture apart from those that contributed to success in war.[2] History, of course, is full of tyrannies, some

of them savage. Though the twentieth century set standards of in-
famy in such matters that would seem difficult if not impossible to
exceed, Assyria could have competed with our worst. The wickedness of Nineveh, Assyria's capital, was no mirage. The thought of
proclaiming the word of God there was for Jonah, as it would have
been for all Hebrews, out of the question. It was no more thinkable
for a Hebrew prophet to proclaim God's word in Nineveh than it
would have been for an inmate of Auschwitz or Bergen Belsen to
preach forgiveness at the Reich's Chancellery in Berlin. Vengeance,
yes; forgiveness, never!

So Jonah flees—and at his own expense. "After paying the
fare, he went aboard and sailed for Tarshish to flee from the Lord."
So much for a plan to save a wicked nation. No sooner is the plot
unveiled than the chief actor hustles off stage.

Jonah was of course not the first—or last—to flee God.

> I fled Him down the nights and down the days;
> I fled Him down the arches of the years;
> I fled Him down the labyrinthine ways
> Of my own mind; and in the midst of tears
> I hid from him.

So writes Francis Thompson in *The Hound of Heaven*. But no
human flight can escape

> . . . those strong Feet that followed, followed after.
> But with unhurrying chase,
> And unperturbed pace,
> Deliberate speed, majestic instancy,
> They beat—and a Voice beat
> More instant than the Feet—
> 'All things betray thee who betrayest Me
> Naught shelters thee, who wilt not shelter Me
> Naught contents thee, who content'st not Me
> All things fly thee, for thou fliest Me. . . .
> Ah, fondest, blindest, weakest!
> I am he Whom thou seekest.'[3]

The Lord is an extremely able combatant. There is to date no record of anyone going nose-to-nose with the Almighty and prevailing—including Jonah. One of the surprising truths of the Bible is that God is not necessarily "nice." This has often been misunderstood. We like to imagine a God who champions our "rights," who exists for the purposes of our self-fulfillment and prosperity—a God who holds people accountable to a standard that differs from their own will, or who demands obedience to a revealed will that confronts and conflicts with their selfish pleasures, is less attractive. We have all heard it said, or perhaps even said it ourselves: "I cannot believe in a God who would allow such things."

Such may be the God we would choose in order to satisfy our wills and lusts. But the God of steadfast love, the Lord of heaven and earth, is not a God of benign neglect, nor does he exist simply to serve our happiness. If the happiness of others is our sole concern, then it is probably safe to say that we care very little for them. We never practice such superficial benevolence toward those for whom we really care—our close friends, children, spouses. Their happiness and self-fulfillment are indeed important to us, but few of us are willing to accept their happiness at the cost of laziness, selfishness, spoiled temperaments, the breaking of covenants, or lack of character. Love wills for the other more than simply happiness.

It is no different with God. Did the older brother think the father likable when he received back his foolish younger brother (Luke 15:11-32)? Did the laborers who got paid the same for working a full day as those who worked an hour find the payment agreeable (Matthew 20:1-16)? No one, I wager, ever thought of the cross of Jesus Christ as nice. But it does reveal the extent of God's love for the world and his willingness to make payment for its evil. Some of God's ways are hard to understand, some perhaps offensive, and some may even cause us, like Jonah, to take flight. God's will is that we know and trust him, that we learn mercy and justice, and that we and those we love—and even those we do not love—find salvation. Such ends are not always served by niceness.

All of which brings us back to Jonah. The remarkable thing about Jonah is that he does not doubt that God is speaking to him. He knows exactly what God has in mind—and he has no inclination to accept it! Tougher than the transformation of the unrighteous is the transformation of the self-righteous. Jonah must first undergo a conversion before he can proclaim one to Nineveh. Ironically, Jonah's conversion begins when he is trying to escape it. The Lord hurls a storm that threatens to break apart the ship in which Jonah is fleeing. Tarshish-or-Bust turns out to be a miniature Nineveh, filled with all sorts of ungodly types. Jonah is apparently the only light on board in a hull-of-a-lot of darkness. Or so it appears.

In reality, however, things are quite different. While righteous Jonah sleeps, the unrighteous sailors pray. While righteous Jonah hides below, the unrighteous strain at the oars above. They pray and work—ora et labora, as the Rule of Benedict prescribes—while Jonah acts the proverbial sluggard. Righteous Jonah desires death; the unrighteous sailors desire his life. The stowaway heedlessly imperils the sailors, whereas they dig their oars into the sea to spare him a justly deserved fate. When their mission is doomed (through no fault of their own), they pray for forgiveness—and they pray not to a pagan deity or "higher power," but to Yahweh, the God of Israel. Jonah vaunts that he is a Hebrew who serves the God of heaven and earth, yet he serves only himself while the pagan sailors serve God on his behalf. The righteous Hebrew grumbles; the unrighteous Gentiles give thanks. Jonah mouths an icy platitude of faith while actually breaking faith; the sailors seek the Lord and are miraculously converted, "greatly fear[ing] the Lord."

The contrasts between Jonah and the pagan sailors are sharp as broken glass, and the consummate storyteller employs them to force us to reconsider our fast and pompous distinctions between righteous and wicked, saved and damned, elect and reprobate. No Gospel writer questioned those same distinctions more than St. Mark. In the first verse of his gospel, Mark declares that Jesus Christ is the Son of God. But not until the crucifixion does it finally dawn on anyone in the story itself who Jesus really is. And who is that someone? Not a disciple, not even Peter. Like Jonah,

the disciples have fled, along with the relatives and associates of
Jesus. Not a Pharisee or member of the Sanhedrin, either. The first
human being in the gospel of Mark to recognize Jesus as the Son
of God is not even a Jew, but a Roman, a "Gentile sinner" as they
were called. In fact, he was the captain of the squad of soldiers that
executed Jesus! "Surely this man was the Son of God!" said the
centurion (Mark 15:39). What an irony for the followers of Jesus to
find that a total outsider—indeed an enemy—was the first person
to see into the heart of the Christian faith!

These surprising ironies continue to our own day. What
Nineveh was to the Israelites, the Soviet Union was to America. The
West built forty-five years of Cold War policy on the premise that
Russia was a ruthless and implacable foe. An entire generation of
Americans was raised in that belief. A thousand NATO resolutions
and trillions of dollars of defense spending were dedicated to that
premise. Our worst case scenario did not transpire, however, and we
pray it never will. Russia revealed a more human face, including a
receptivity to the gospel, not unlike the receptivity of Nineveh.

But perhaps we have been unfair to Jonah. After all, at the
height of the storm he spits out a confession: "Throw me into the
sea . . . and it will become calm. I know that it is my fault that
this great storm has come upon you." Surely this reveals at least a
modicum of character and nobility in Jonah's soul, a final tenderness before a tragic end.

Look again. Jonah's prayer is a death wish, not a confession. He
is no closer to submitting to God's will than he was before the storm,
nor is he concerned about the lives of the sailors. What seems like
tenderness of spirit is in truth the last bullet of hardened defiance.

When I was in college I spent a summer traveling through
Europe with two friends. Toward the end of our trip we visited
Paris and attended the play *The Chairs* by Eugene Ionesco. It was
a perfect production for three nonFrancophone collegians like
ourselves, because there was virtually no speaking in the play. The
play has only two characters, a man and his wife. Old and dying,
the man decides to write down what he has learned in life for pos-
terity. Sensing the gravity of the event, his wife brings in chairs to

accommodate the audience of his final testament. She brings in ten chairs . . . twenty-five . . . fifty . . . two hundred chairs—hence, the play's name. All the while the man writes feverishly. At last, the speech is finished and the hearers seated. The old man rises to the podium, raises the script . . . and just as he begins to speak, he sputters and dies! With the corpse in center stage, the curtain fell and applause broke forth.

I was stunned by the play's icy nihilism. The problem of existence, says Ionesco, a French existentialist, is that life sends us mixed signals. As humans, we have longings for hope, justice, peace, goodness—for meaning—but these longings find no correspondence in the world of reality. Our sense of beauty is starved by functional uniformity and monotonous utility; truth is twisted by lies and intrigue; justice is bludgeoned by senseless brutality. Life, in other words, is despair, and the only fitting response to the ruinous contradiction between longing and reality, maintain the existentialists, is to die in protest and defiance. Hence, the ending to *The Chairs*: even if you could solve the riddle of the universe, you would kick off before uttering a word of it.

Jonah and Ionesco are in the same boat—although Jonah's despair is in some ways worse because it is brought on not by a meaningless world but by a personal God. Whenever someone like Jonah slips to the brink of such an abyss, there can be no rescue unless it comes from God. That is one of the two central points of the book of Jonah: God's saving a proud and mutinous prophet from his own destruction. It is a counteroffensive of grace in the face of despair.

The Lord rescues his headstrong prophet by several "appointments." The chief appointment is a big fish that the Lord commands to swallow Jonah. But as it turns out, Jonah is indigestible, which tells us that God spares believers from certain evils in order to employ them for greater purposes. Hence, the fish is appointed to vomit Jonah out on dry land. Aboard the ship Jonah had bragged that his God was Lord of sea and land; he now understands that article of faith in a new way. This truth is enshrined in the architecture of certain churches in Silesia and Bohemia, where the pulpit is built to resemble a whale's opened mouth. Whale pulpits, as they are called, are accessible only by climbing through the fish's body—symbolizing that the preacher cannot proclaim the word of God except from the mouth of deliverance.

God has still further appointments for Jonah. He appoints a vine to shade Jonah, a worm to remove the vine, and an east wind to blast Jonah. All these appointments—some advantageous, others chastening—remind Jonah that he lives solely by grace.

Jonah paid dear money for his outbound flight, but God returns him to land free of charge. The fugitive now finds himself high and dry back at square one, where "the word of the Lord came to Jonah a second time: 'Go to the great city of Nineveh and proclaim to it the message I give you.'" Jonah is the only prophet in the Bible who receives the call of God twice. That too is a sign of God's grace.

And so, the reluctant prophet goes. The worst possible thing happens, however: Nineveh believes the word of God and repents. We are given no explanation for this unprecedented turn of events—except, of course, that the hand of God is in it. Jonah's surely is not. His message is as devoid of grace as a hot poker. If only our enemies were as wicked in reality as we make them out to be in our minds. We could then justify the most extreme measures against them. But that is seldom the case—even in a people as devoid of virtue as the Assyrians. Far from a sporadic conversion, Nineveh undergoes wholesale repentance, "from the greatest to the least." Even the cows repent, we are told. That is an unusually successful revival. How many people reckon with the possibility that the livestock of their enemies are precious to God? Not Jonah.

Jonah is not the first (or the last) to discover that God sometimes uses a message differently than the prophet intends it. In Hebrew Jonah's name means "dove," but he preaches vengeance like a hawk: "Forty more days and Nineveh will be overturned." Nineveh will indeed be overturned, but much differently than Jonah expects. The prophet hopes to sink Nineveh's eight ball, but God puts a different spin on Jonah's game, resulting in quite a different table position.

Centuries later the apostle Paul remembered as he sat in jail that evangelists and preachers do not control the effects of their message (Philippians 1:15-18). The word of God is, after all, God's word, not ours. It has a life of its own. People who preach Christ from selfish ambition or false motives are often surprised by the good that results. Every preacher or Sunday school teacher can tell you of parishioners who learned from them lessons they did not intentionally teach. There once was a man who set out to write a book disproving the historicity of the resurrection of Jesus— and was himself converted by the evidence he uncovered. Frank Morison's *Who Moved the Stone?* is a classic reminder that human intentions do not determine God's sovereign plan.[4]

Jonah and God are at loggerheads: Jonah wills the destruction of Nineveh, and God wills its salvation. As one enters the Sistine Chapel in Rome, one's attention is drawn to Michelangelo's commanding figure on the front wall—Jesus in the Last Judgment, right arm raised in wrath. The arm of Jesus actually points to a much larger figure on the vault of the ceiling of the Sistine Chapel where the Last Judgment converges with Michelangelo's scenes of Genesis. That figure is Jonah, recoiling as though condemned by Christ's arm of judgment below—or by surprise at the prospects of new creation above. There sits the prophet, suspended between death and life, between judgment and grace.

Judgment or grace, death or life—that is Jonah's predicament. Like the return of a bad dream, the repentance of Nineveh is the last straw for Jonah. It was bad enough that the sailors had repented; now, inexplicably, the Ninevites follow suit. And repentance from the top down, no less. What began with the captain at sea continues with the king at Nineveh. The most notorious of kings has become a paragon of virtue!

Like Jonah, we portray our enemies in sinister shapes in order to justify our behavior toward them. Also like Jonah, we find it hard to conceive that what we detest in our enemies might actually be present in us. What the apostle Paul teaches in Romans 2:1 is the book of Jonah reduced to a single pronouncement: "You, therefore, have no excuse, you who pass judgment on someone

else, for at whatever point you judge the other, you are condemning yourself, because you who pass judgment do the same things."
I was forced to face this sober truth not long ago. Like many
people, I was shocked by the catastrophe on Mount Everest in May
1996 in which a dozen mountaineers perished. One of the most
disturbing sideshows in that circus of tragedies was the story of
two Japanese climbers who in their summit bid bypassed three in-
jured, starving, and freezing climbers. The Japanese had sufficient
provisions to render aid to the stranded climbers, but they did not
want to jeopardize their ascent by stopping to assist them. As a
result, all three climbers died. Later, when asked why they had not
stopped to help, one of the climbers said, "We were too tired to
help. Above 8,000 meters [26,000 feet] is not a place where people
can afford morality."[5]

The actions of the two climbers and the statement attempting
to justify them were, in my judgment, a callous and contemptible
example of egoism. On a number of occasions I retold the story
in my preaching and teaching to illustrate the true face of egoistic
ethics, base and unjustifiable—and doubly so in the mountains,
where the dangers inherent in climbing should make all climbers
their brothers' keepers.

A few years later, while leading a college study tour to the
Middle East, I was hiking up Mount Sinai in the darkness before
dawn in order to be on the summit at sunrise. The hike up 7,500-
foot Mount Sinai is tame in comparison to Mount Everest, where
oxygen deprivation impairs physical exertion and judgment itself. As my students and I neared the top of Mount Sinai we were
passed by two Bedouins carrying a man down the mountain. The
man was unconscious. His sporadic breathing, rattled and gur-
gling, indicated he was in critical condition. He was, I suspected,
suffering from pulmonary edema, a malady of mountaineering
caused by ascending too rapidly. Pulmonary edema is fatal unless
the climber affected is taken rapidly to a lower altitude. For a brief
moment I considered halting my ascent and helping the Bedouins
carry the man down the mountain. But my desire to make it to the
top checked my impulse. Without further thought, I gave one of

the Bedouins my flashlight and continued upward. They seemed to be doing all right by themselves, I assured my uneasy conscience.

The sunrise from the summit was glorious, but it was over-shadowed by what transpired on the way down. Not far below the place where we had passed the Bedouins, a figure draped with a blanket was lying on the ground. Two shoes protruded from under the blanket. The man carried by the Bedouins was dead. Whether he died while being carried down, or was put down and died, I do not know. I do know, however, that every step down the mountain smote my conscience. What I had found so loathsome in the two Japanese climbers on Everest had been essentially repeated in my own action on Mount Sinai.

That is the message of the book of Jonah. What Jonah detests in Nineveh is present in himself. If only Jonah can see that his heart is as contrary to God as is the heart of Nineveh: "There is no one righteous, not even one" (Romans 3:10). If only he can see that the grace extended to the Ninevites is the same grace extended to him: "The Lord is good to all; he has compassion on all he has made" (Psalm 145:9).

The climax of the book of Jonah comes at the very end, where, for the first time, the angry prophet speaks to God. His displeasure is expressed in bitter eloquence: "O Lord, is this not what I said when I was still at home? That is why I was so quick to flee to Tarshish. I knew that you are a gracious and compassionate God, slow to anger and abounding in love, a God who relents from sending calamity. Now, O Lord, take away my life, for it is better for me to die than to live." At last, Jonah's cards are on the table. He has resisted God's intrusion since word one because he feared all along that God would forgive Nineveh rather than judge it. And now that the effect of God's intrusion is fully evident, he would rather die than accept it! How unmistakably like the parable of the prodigal son (Luke 15:11-32). The worthless younger brother—or Nineveh—is easier to convert than the righteous older brother, who is so much like Jonah. Angry and sullen, the older brother refuses to join the celebration, blaming his father for throwing a party for a son who squandered his property on prostitutes. How deserving vengeance seemed, how unfair grace.

We all know how Jonah feels, even if we are not so brave as to hazard admitting it. Think of it this way: Suppose you were to die tonight and go to heaven. Would there be anyone you would be grieved to see there? The office partner who got the promotion you thought you deserved, even though he was phony as a form letter? The undeserving kid who got the full-tuition scholarship you worked so hard for? The spouse who betrayed you? The unscrupulous real estate agent who defrauded you? The debtor who refused to pay up? Don't laugh too quickly at Jonah's tirade against grace. He is not alone. There is no getting around it: grace is the most offensive part of the gospel.

The king of Nineveh sits in the ashes of repentance; Jonah sits in the cool shade of judgment: "Jonah went out and sat down at a place east of the city." Jonah preaches vengeance "a day's journey" into the city (the ancient equivalent of midtown during rush hour), but the thought of grace sends him to the outskirts of town in depression. God is as patient with Jonah's self-righteousness as he has been with Nineveh's wickedness; he reaches for the heart of this troubled soul, if it can be reached at all. Jonah and Nineveh have traded places. The inability to repent, which Jonah all along ascribed to Nineveh, is his own inability as well; the grace that Jonah begrudges Nineveh is the very grace by which Jonah is being sustained!

The story concludes with two questions to Jonah—and to us as readers. "Have you any right to be angry?" asks God. Are we who are raised with a particular view of the world to blame God for having a broader view? If we accuse God of being soft on our enemies, might not our enemies accuse God of being soft on us? Are our judgments the final truth in the universe, or do we preserve God's right to act independently of us? Shall we believe the best of ourselves and the worst of others? Are there excuses to be made for our behavior but none to be made for the behavior of others? Are the outcries over our enemies' crimes based on the same degree of understanding as are the pleas for God's mercy on our own? Who is God, after all? Is Jonah God, or is God God?

The second great question is, "Should I not be concerned about that great city?" This phrase finds a close parallel in God's word about Corinth to the apostle Paul, which the original Greek might be translated, "for the people in that city are important to me" (Acts 18:10). How ironic that two of the most infamous cities in history—Nineveh and Corinth—are precious to God! God does not simply show kindness and mercy to the deserving. God's unfathomable grace goes out to the undeserving, transforming enemies into friends, opponents into partners. Jonah is forced to confess, "You are El-chanown," in Hebrew (4:2), "a God supremely compassionate." This is why God relents his judgment and showers compassion on Nineveh (3:10). God's treatment of Nineveh is simply an extension of his gracious nature. The final verse of Jonah ends with the haunting question, "Should I not be concerned about that great city" (4:11)? The Hebrew word for "concerned," *chus*, literally means "eyes filled with tears." What moves Jonah to hardened defiance moves God to tears.

These two questions conclude the book of Jonah. What finally happens to the angry prophet? Does he repent and accept the will of God—and with it the joy and freedom of God? We are not told. His last recorded word is "I am angry enough to die." We hope it was not his last word. The book of Jonah thus ends like the parable of the prodigal son, to which we referred earlier. We do not know if Jonah or the older brother submitted to the Father's will, and there is a reason for that. The storytellers cannot end the stories without our participation, for the stories are not ultimately about an ancient Hebrew prophet or an invidious older brother, but about us. It is we who must supply the ending. Will we bind God by our judgments, or will we free God to transform our enemies—even ourselves—by grace?

QUESTIONS FOR DISCUSSION

1. If "grace is the most offense part of the gospel," what makes it so offensive?

2. Name a Nineveh or Assyria for modern-day Christians? How do our attitudes mirror Jonah's?

3. Discuss the similar irony of the pagan sailors and their encounter with Jonah, and the Roman guard at the cross of Jesus?

4. How would you respond to the question, "If you died tonight would it grieve you to see a particular individual in heaven?"

5. What do you find encouraging by the fact that God called Jonah twice to go to Nineveh?

6

God of the Impossible

In the sixth month, God sent the angel Gabriel to Nazareth, a town in Galilee, to a virgin pledged to be married to a man named Joseph, a descendant of David. The virgin's name was Mary. The angel went to her and said, "Greetings, you who are highly favored! The Lord is with you."

Mary was greatly troubled at his words and wondered what kind of greeting this might be. But the angel said to her, "Do not be afraid, Mary, you have found favor with God. You will be with child and give birth to a son, and you are to give him the name Jesus. He will be great and will be called the Son of the Most High. The Lord God will give him the throne of his father David, and he will reign over the house of Jacob forever; his kingdom will never end."

"How will this be," Mary asked the angel, "since I am a virgin?"

The angel answered, "The Holy Spirit will come upon you, and the power of the Most High will overshadow you. So the holy one to be born will be called the Son of God. Even Elizabeth your relative is going to have a child in her old age, and she who was said to be barren is in her sixth month. For nothing is impossible with God."

"I am the Lord's servant," Mary answered. "May it be to me as you have said." Then the angel left her.

—Luke 1:26-38

IN IMAGINARY WORKS IT is difficult to make virtuous characters as believable and attractive as bad characters. The villains of literature and screen—Captain Ahab, the boys who go bad in Lord of the Flies, Darth Vader, Norman Bates, Hannibal the Cannibal—are all, as a rule, larger figures, more gripping and more memorable, than are the heroes and heroines of even the same authors and producers. This is as true of religious literature as it is of secular literature. In Paradise Lost, Milton's Satan has all the good lines, but who remembers a word of his Christ? Dante's *The Divine Comedy* is one of the great masterpieces of world literature, yet literary critics as well as college freshmen rarely read The Paradiso, and those who do usually judge its virtue and bliss flat and insipid compared to the gargoyled vices of *The Inferno*.

There is a good reason why this is so. Human nature stands closer to evil than to good. Intrigue, scheming, and deception are more instinctual to us than love, goodness, and forgiveness. The vices are "first nature," so to speak, whereas virtue is "second nature," either a learned response or no response at all. It is easier to figure out ways to cheat the IRS than to solve the problems of hunger or violence. When we are wronged we can hatch ten brilliant schemes of revenge; but try to devise even a paltry plan for redeeming a bad situation. Dostoyevsky thus had an easier task in creating Raskolnikov, the brooding ax-killer of *Crime and Punishment*, than he did in creating Alyosha, the only virtuous figure in a family of miscreants in *The Brothers Karamazov*. This is not to diminish Raskolnikov; he is a powerful figure of darkness and depravity. It is simply to say that it is harder to make Alyosha as scintillatingly good as Raskolnikov is bad. And it is nearly impossible to conceive of a world in which the reverse would be true. Perhaps the angels in heaven have more trouble depicting bad characters than they do good characters. We do not know, of course, if angels write novels, but we do know that they stand closer to God than we do.

These reflections on fictional characters may help us as we think about Mary. Mary is harder to bring to "life" than are the other participants in the divine colloquy or conversation because she possesses a simplicity and sincerity that they lack. Abraham, Jacob, Gideon, and Jonah are more accessible to us because they are complex characters. We are surprised to learn that they and other characters like them in the Bible have questions, fears, and struggles with God. In their struggles we see some of our own reflected, and we are comforted in knowing that if there is hope for them there may also be hope for us. But the very compromises and flaws that draw these characters close to us are lacking in Mary. Her trusting receptivity of God's will puts her in a different league from most mortals who struggle with the elements of faith. Mary is easily stereotyped as a mannequin of piety, removed and perhaps even alienated from us, and her distance can also conceal her genuine experience of God from us.

Mary's patina and aura are truly ironic because, of all the characters in this book, she is the least likely from a human perspective to have been called by God. Were Mary's call not so familiar as a Christmas story, its jarring ironies would shock us—like grabbing an electrical wire with the current on. God calls unlikely people, but none is as unlikely as Mary. The Annunciation of the Jewish Messiah comes not in the land of the Jews but in "Galilee of the Gentiles," to quote Matthew (4:15). The Messiah who will consummate the throne of David will not be born of royalty but of peasants. He will fulfill the promise to Jacob; but Joseph, the paternal link to Jacob's lineage, is only the father apparent—"so it was thought" (Luke 3:23)—the true father being God begetting through a common peasant woman. Finally, the one born of Mary will fulfill the covenant of Israel, yet the Annunciation comes to a young woman who at the time is not even in the covenant of marriage.

Ironically, Mary's place in God's plan is quite disproportionate to her status in Galilean society. So important is the Annunciation that the divine communiqué is entrusted not to a potentate, ruler, prophet, or sage, not even to an angel, but to the most preeminent of angels, the archangel Gabriel. Nothing of the "to-whom-it-may-concern" mentality here. Gabriel is personally commissioned by God Almighty and sent to this particular place and to this particular woman. It would be hard to find another historical figure so marginal by temporal standards yet so honored by eternal standards. The first words of the Magnificat reveal that Mary understands the unparalleled irony of her election: "God has looked on the tapeinosis (Greek, meaning "the low, humble, earthy condition") of his maidservant" (Luke 1:48, my translation).

Shortly before he was executed in a Nazi prison, Dietrich Bonhoeffer wrote an Advent poem about God's wondrous conspiracy and circumvention of human power in choosing Mary. The poem is entitled "Where God Wants to Be."

> Where the understanding is outraged,
> where human nature rebels,
> where our piety keeps a nervous distance:
> there, precisely there, God loves to be;
> there he baffles the wisdom of the wise;
> there he vexes our nature, our religious instincts.
> There he wants to be, and no one can prevent him.
> Only the humble believe him and rejoice
> that God is so free and grand,
> that he works wonders where man loses heart,
> that he makes splendid what is slight and lowly.
> Indeed, this is the wonder of wonders,
> that God loves the lowly.
> 'God has regarded the low estate of his handmaiden.'
> God in lowliness—
> that is the revolutionary, the passionate word of Advent.[1]

How utterly astonishing that the Lord of heaven, whose glory surpasses all creation as the brightness of the sun exceeds the night stars, should share the lot of the lowly on earth. Yet that is where God wants to be. How unlike where we want to be. We want to be in the winner's circle. We want to be recognized, appreciated, applauded. We find luxury easy to adjust to. But God's driving love and passion, as Bonhoeffer so clearly captures, seeks out and sides with the common, the needy, the destitute. With Mary, there God wants to be.

A woman of such low rank can scarcely presume upon God. Hence, Gabriel must initiate the conversation. In Mary's day and place a woman would normally address her husband only in private, and she was forbidden by law from addressing a rabbi in public. At least ten Jewish males were required to procure a rabbi and synagogue, and it would appear that Nazareth barely qualified. Archaeological evidence indicates that the town where Jesus grew up was a poor hamlet of cave dwellings chopped into a rocky hillside. The extent of the town was no more than sixty acres, perhaps fifty families in number. The insignificance of Nazareth is sealed by its silence in the Jewish tradition. It is nowhere mentioned in the Old Testament, in Josephus, in the Midrash, or in the Talmud. In the New Testament, Nazareth is mentioned only a dozen times, and outside the New Testament its first mention is by an obscure writer, Julius Africanus, a full two centuries after Jesus' birth. By all indicators, Nazareth was humble, unpretentious, and unimportant.

How paradoxical that the word of God would come to such a place—and to a poor, young, unmarried woman in it. Anyone who has lived in rural America can appreciate the utter unlikelihood of this scene. Rural is synonymous with powerlessness; it means to be divorced from the centers of importance and influence. People who live in rural America are reminded day in and day out that history, change, and the future happen elsewhere. It was no different in Mary's day. How utterly remarkable that here, in Nazareth, God announces the salvation of the world. Not to Rome or Byzantium or Alexandria, not to Paris or Tokyo or Los Angeles, but to Nowheresville God dispatches the highest prince in creation. Nazareth was the kind of place people told jokes about: "It may not be the end of the world, but you can see it from there!" In this dusty hillside settlement, bypassed by people on their way to places that really mattered—Caesarea, Sepphoris, Tiberius, and Damascus—God deigns to bring forth the most influential person in all history. From now to eternity, forgotten and insignificant

Nazareth overturns the tables of power and topples every human scale of importance. This is the place where the God of the cosmos put in a personal appearance. How true the observation of New Testament scholar Eduard Schweizer: "God is precisely God in that he can do what humanity cannot do: he can allow himself to be rejected, he can be made low and of no consequence—without, however, like humanity, being plunged into an inferiority complex, which shows that humanity with all its heart wants to be great."[2]

In Nazareth and nowhere else the clarion announcement is heard: "Greetings, you who are highly favored! The Lord is with you." Why Mary? Why should this simple, inauspicious girl be favored by God? We are not told, for instance, as we are of Zechariah and Elizabeth, the parents of John the Baptist (Luke 1:6), that Mary is righteous and blameless. The New Testament is surprisingly devoid of details about Mary, in fact, leaving a sparse bottom line about her character. The language of the Annunciation suggests that Mary's choosing lies solely in the mystery of God's grace. The Greek word behind "highly favored" is in the same word-family as the word for "grace." In the New Testament, grace is used solely of divine acts, not of human merit. It characterizes God's sovereign freedom to bestow kindness and mercy on people who do not expect them and could never deserve them. The grammatical form of the Greek word translated "highly favored" indicates that grace is imputed to Mary, and thus the result of God's choosing rather than of her worthiness or merit.

Favored! Object of grace! Who ever thinks of the poor as favored? The poor and powerless hear of relocation settlements, land exchanges, labor camps, servitude, pillage, plunder, prison, war, and taxes. No one favors the poor because no one has to. They exist on the margins of society as its most defenseless members.

My first experience with the poor came in the late 1960s when my wife and I worked with street kids in Morningside Heights in New York City. Later, as a pastor, I served on a citizens' committee, consisting of experts on urban affairs and representatives from various sectors of society, to address the concern of urban deterioration. As our committee discussed "cleaning up the inner city" and "doing something about violence," I was struck by the way our attempts to objectify problems eclipsed the people who were caught in such problems, and might well result in new injustices to them. It is not that such endeavors are mean-spirited or unsympathetic. They may be well meaning, as ours were, perhaps even self-sacrificing. But in our concern for "the disadvantaged" we could easily transgress the people we were trying to help by depriving them of the power and responsibility essential to humanness.

People fear growing old or becoming disabled for the same reason they fear poverty. They fear the loss of personhood, they fear not being told the truth of their condition, they fear no longer being able to make choices over themselves and their property, they fear becoming a statistic in a study. An experiment among both the urban and rural poor of Latin America has in the past few decades attempted an alternative to the welfare concept of charity and the disenfranchisement that it entails. Christian Base Communities, as they are called, have sought to restore a vital Christian witness in society by refraining from doing something for the poor, concentrating rather on enabling the poor to understand their experience, name it, and decide what the gospel would call them to do about it.

Mary personifies such disenfranchisement and powerlessness. Given this fact, we might expect her to welcome a divine visitation in hopes of an improvement in her status. But like the other initiatives of the Divine Intruder in this book, Gabriel's word is not a welcome word. Luke tells us the Annunciation comes to Mary not as a comforting and consoling word but as something that disrupts her world, disturbing and frightening her. The Muslim Quran says this was because the angel appeared as "a full-grown man" and frightened Mary.[3] Mary's fear, however, stems from something other than being startled by a strange man. If you know anything about the Bible you know that the inevitable response of human beings to angelic appearances is fear, terror, even dread. There are five stories in the Bible of angels announcing births, and in each birth—Ishmael, Isaac, Samson, John the Baptist, and Jesus—the mothers-to-be (or father-to-be in the case of John the Baptist) respond in fear and prostration before the angelic visitant. It is a perfectly natural response, if you think about it. I shall never forget the first time I was aware of being followed by the Stasi, the secret police, in communist East Germany. My heart rate spiked. How much more confounding an appearance of the all-knowing Eternal, holy and consuming, at your office desk or kitchen counter?

The purpose of Gabriel's visitation is not the glorification of Mary. Once Mary has been greeted by Gabriel, the remainder of the Annunciation focuses on the birth and mission of the Messiah who will be born from her. She will conceive; she will bear a son; his name will be called Jesus, meaning "God's salvation"; he will be mighty, the Son of the Highest; God will give to him the throne of his father David; he will rule over the house of Jacob forever; his kingdom will have no end. Mary immediately understands that the focus of Gabriel's message is Jesus. And by her response we know that she sees herself as a recipient of grace. Becoming the mother of the Messiah is not something she has earned; rather, God imputes the honor to her by sheer grace.

Grace is the most essential and—as we have seen with Jonah—the most scandalous truth in all the Bible. It is at once the simplest and yet most difficult reality of the gospel to understand and accept. It means God's unwarranted love for us in spite of who and what we are. It means there is no merit that will earn us what God wants to give us. When we look at the sacrificial love of Christ's death for us on the cross and God's forgiveness of our sins through it, we can never say that such love was something we deserved by virtue of our good character or good will or good works. Grace is unmerited. Period.

The choice of an unwed peasant girl in remote Nazareth to become the mother of the Messiah is a supreme expression of grace. For a woman to be unwed in the Jewish society of her day was to be severed from the rights and powers that Jewish law afforded through men, whether as fathers, husbands, or sons. Mary stands in a no-man's land—no longer subject to her father, not yet subject to her husband. In the vulnerable transition from one to the other, God intervenes in an offensive of grace.

Can you remember when you were a kid on the school play-ground and it came time to choose sides for a game? Who got chosen first—and who was left until last? The kids who could knock the ball over the fence were chosen first; the kids with skinny legs and drooping socks were left till the end. The leftovers were never really chosen, but simply divided between sides and relegated to positions that would not affect the game. In the Roman occupation of Palestine, Mary is one of the leftovers. She enjoys no privilege or favored status in Nazareth; why should she with God? But she does! The angel addresses Mary by name. She is not the object of a divine form letter or heavenly telemarketing. She is for God a unique person, and it is to her as a person, not simply to her situation, that God speaks.

The reasons for grace are profound and inexhaustible. Why God chooses Mary we do not know, but that she is favored we cannot deny. This observation, as simple as it is profound, is one of the sterling truths of the Bible, that God is for us (Romans 8:31). Not angry with us, not waiting to get even with us, not judging us, and above all, not oblivious or indifferent to us. God is for us—a simple prepositional phrase that is the blueprint of salvation. Mary is the first participant in the divine–human conversation to take that prepositional phrase at face value. It changed not only her life, but all history. It can do something similar to and through you.

It is quite remarkable that God should be for us. We have done everything imaginable to shut the God who made the world and everything in it out of our lives. As a young pastor I once received a visit from a Vietnam veteran whose wife, having lived well enough without him while he was gone, decided she did not want him back. The vet was devastated. He buried his head in his hands and trembled with grief. "The thing that kept me alive in 'Nam was the thought of seeing my wife and child again. And now the lock has been changed on the door to my own house, and I've been shut out of my own family," he cried. As I listened to him I thought, That is God's story too. That is exactly what we have done to God in our world. We have changed the locks and barred the doors. As the gospel of John tells it, ". . . and though the world was made through him, the world did not recognize him. He came to that which was his own, but his own did not receive him" (John 1:10-11).

One of the most famous paintings of Jesus shows him knocking submissively on a door. In reality, God usually needs to take more assertive measures to gain entrance into our lives. He must intrude where he is unwanted and unwelcome. He must make surprise and incognito appearances. He must, like a Christian artist I know who received federal funding for a painting, disguise the gospel so that it is not immediately apparent, lest it be rejected out of hand.

If God is to accomplish his will in our sorry and sordid world, he must go to lengths that exceed anything humanly imaginable. Jesus once told a parable about a landowner who lent his vineyard to tenant farmers (Mark 12:1-12). At harvest time he sent his servants to collect his due. Power went to the tenants' heads, however, and they paid their rent in blows when the servants arrived. The landowner sent more servants, and they received the same or worse treatment. Some were beaten, some driven off, some killed. The landowner finally decided to send his son, his only son, whom he loved. "Surely they will honor my son," he said (see verse 6). Send your son? we gasp! Send in the militia, send the Get-Even-Team, but don't send your beloved son! But that is exactly what God does. Such is the extent and depth of the divine intrusion into our world.

John Milton included a poignant conversation near the end of *Paradise Lost* that captures the radical risk of the Divine Intruder. Eve, perceiving the enormity of evil that will befall the world because of sin, suggests to Adam that they check the spread of evil by not bearing children.

> If care of our descent perplex us most,
> Which must be born to certain woe, devoured
> By Death at last, and miserable it is
> To be to others cause of misery,
> Our own begotten, and of our loins to bring
> Into this cursed World a woeful Race,
> That after wretched Life must be at last
> Food for so foul a Monster, in thy power

It lies, yet ere conception to prevent
The Race unblest, to being yet unbegot.
Childless thou art, Childless remain:
So Death shall be deceaved his glut, and with us two
Be forced to satisfy his Ravenous Maw.[4]

Eve's decision makes perfect sense from a human perspective: no more offspring, no further spread of sin. But Milton has the archangel Gabriel inform Eve of the fatal flaw in her plan: without offspring, there can be no salvation. Adam and Eve stand before a terrible dilemma: sin will have to spread farther and deeper before a savior will come to redeem the world from it. It is like being told a disease will have to infect your whole body before the cure will take effect.

Milton's dialogue is, of course, hypothetical, but it succeeds in setting the Annunciation to Mary in the long strain of salvation history. The Annunciation has, by God's sovereign design and work, been in preparation even before the first human transgression—from all eternity, in fact. The Annunciation is finally the answer to the world's woes. The banishment of Eve now yields to the blessing in Mary; the hope for which the world has groaned in agony rests in her womb. "The whole world," said Bernard of Clairvaux in a homily "In Praise of the Virgin Mother," "waits for Mary's reply."[5]

Gabriel announces to Mary, "You will be with child and give birth to a son, and you are to give him the name Jesus." Mary's task is not simply to be a surrogate womb for God, however. She must respond to the wonderful and bewildering news of Gabriel with more than physical relinquishment. She must respond with faith, because faith is the only response that we can make to grace.

I once observed a guide in a European art museum call attention to a medieval painting in which the Annunciation was depicted as though it were a laser beam from the Holy Spirit to Mary's ear. With a condescending smile the guide explained that the painting was the result of a failure to understand the facts of procreation, or, at the least, that it was a euphemistic concession to a sexually naïve age. The guide was actually quite mistaken. The

NB

old painters—for whom the Annunciation was as important for salvation as the crucifixion—on occasion portrayed the virginal conception occurring not in Mary's womb but in her ear. They knew well enough how women got pregnant. Their depiction of the Annunciation was informed by more than biology, however. The crux of the Annunciation, as their paintings rightly reveal, was not simply a biological transfusion but a response of hearing and trust in the consummate promise of God.

And so the hope of the ages, the Messiah of David, will be born of Mary. Mary predictably and reasonably questions, "How will this be, since I am a virgin?" Mary's response is a world apart from Sarah's derision, Moses' excuses, Gideon's complaints, and Jonah's flight. Mary is not resisting; she is simply in a quandary. She knows what our age has chosen to forget, that sexual intercourse and childbearing belong within a marital relationship. Despite all her familiarity to us, Mary is, as we have noted, the most foreign personality in the divine colloquy; and in no respect is she more foreign to our age than in her commitment to sexual holiness.

It would be gross naïveté to imagine that the first-century Mediterranean world shared Mary's chasteness. The sexual scandals of the Roman emperors or, closer to Mary's home in Nazareth, of the Herodian family make modern-day pornography look passé. The Roman biographer and historian Suetonius described in his writings the sexual depravity of Tiberius, the Roman emperor under whom Jesus was crucified, and it is so outrageous that modern editors often refuse to translate the original Latin into English.[6] And Tiberius's depravity was no worse than that of Roman emperors before and after him. In Jewish Nazareth, Mary may have been isolated from the worst excesses of Roman sexual abandonment, but she was not isolated from human nature, or from the power that men—including Jewish men in some circumstances—enjoyed over the bodies of women and slaves. The several instances in the Gospels where Jesus is in the presence of prostitutes or women of ill-repute are testimony to more than one sexual standard in the world in which Mary was raised. In her transparent question, "How will this be, since I am a virgin?"

Mary testifies to her understanding that God has a revealed will regarding sexual expression, and that it does not include intercourse outside marriage.

This is one reason she is so confounded by Gabriel's announcement. The God who instituted childbearing within the confines of marriage appears to be contravening his own commandment by authorizing the birth of the Messiah to an unmarried woman. The Annunciation of Mary stands as a reminder that faith is always more than morality. There is a movement afoot today to reduce the Christian faith to "character," to a code of ethics more or less the same as the ethics of other faiths. Character and morality are safer than faith because they lie within our control. Character is something we can all agree on because of its obvious importance for the endurance of civilization. Character is rational, whereas faith requires belief in God or the supernatural. Character is a work we can do and for which we can receive credit, whereas faith demands that we worship and adore something beyond ourselves. A person can develop the most virtuous character in the world and still be a rebel against God. Christianity is indeed ethical, passionately so, but Christianity is always more than ethics. Had Mary followed the dictates of character and morality, she would not have become the mother of the Messiah. Gabriel's pronouncement comes to Mary not as a call to moral behavior but as a call to radical trust in the word of God. In this instance, in fact, the call to trust runs counter to God's moral order.

No thinker, perhaps, struggled with the distinction between faith and ethics more than Søren Kierkegaard, the nineteenth-century Danish theologian. In *Fear and Trembling*, Kierkegaard discusses the scandalous predicament of Abraham who understands God to command him to do an inherently immoral act, to kill his son Isaac (Genesis 22:1-19). Abraham, says Kierkegaard, must choose between the universal—that which is ethical under normal circumstances—and the particular call of God in the present situation. In the vast majority of instances, to be sure, God's will and the ethical are the same, but in certain limited and extreme instances they may differ, as they did for Abraham and as they do for Mary.

In such instances the choice of faith must suspend the ethical principle momentarily in order to obey God, a dilemma Kierkegaard calls "the teleological suspension of the ethical." The teleological suspension of the ethical is the setting aside of a principle, even a moral principle, when it conflicts with the concrete word of God.[7]

It would be an extremely rare circumstance that an act of faith would include killing another person, as it did for Abraham, but that does not render the teleological suspension of the ethical moot for modern believers. During World War II Christians in German-occupied Europe discovered that if they were to defend and harbor Jews, for instance, they had to break the laws of God by lying to authorities, stealing ration cards, and so on. Dietrich Bonhoeffer, whose poem we quoted earlier, wrestled profoundly with this problem. Bonhoeffer understood that Christ's love for real people led him to take the burden of their guilt upon himself. In following Jesus Christ in freedom and responsibility, Bonhoeffer further understood that he too must be willing to incur guilt for the sake of others. If he absented himself from the evil descending on Germany in the Nazi period in order to remain moral, then he would not be following God's will. But if he followed God's will and entered the fray, then he must, in some instances, sacrifice his morality and incur guilt.[8]

In our own day the teleological suspension of the ethical has presented itself to believers who have felt obliged to commit acts of civil disobedience for the sake of human rights. The breaking of moral principles in the name of faith obviously raises a number of serious questions, and it is no accident that it has provoked vigorous controversy in the history of Christian thought. One of the conclusions of that debate, incidentally, is that the teleological suspension of the ethical is more likely to be justifiable, if it can be justified at all, when its objective is the benefit of others rather than of self. When its beneficiary is primarily or exclusively self, it is far less likely to be the will of God.

Mary alone must respond to God's call, but she is not left alone to fulfill it. With the call comes God's equipping for the task. God gives to Mary—as God gives to every believer—the overshadowing and empowering presence of the Holy Spirit to enable her to fulfill his holy call. "The Holy Spirit will come upon you," says Gabriel, "and the power of the Most High will overshadow you. So the holy one to be born will be called the Son of God."

Mary will be prepared for her holy calling by three manifestations of the Almighty: the Holy Spirit will be sent to her, the power of the Most High God will overshadow her, and the Son of God will be conceived within her. The word for "overshadowing" is the same word used in the Greek Old Testament for the overshadowing of the tabernacle with God's presence (Exodus 40:35). It is also the same word used of the overshadowing of Jesus at the Transfiguration (Mark 9:7). In all three instances the overshadowing signifies the filling with God's presence and equipping for God's purpose. In the virginal conception, Mary, the young peasant woman of Nazareth, becomes the living tabernacle of God. Whenever any believer submits humbly and obediently to the will of God, there too is the living manifestation of God; there too God does the impossible in our lives.

Mary is empowered not by male sperm, but by the Holy Spirit of God. The child born of her will not be called Joseph's son but God's Son. In a rare subterfuge of history, the almighty male is relegated to the sidelines. Sojourner Truth, the nineteenth-century emancipated slave who became a religious visionary, aptly captured the divine offense of the Incarnation: "That man say we can't have as much rights as a man 'cause Christ wasn't a woman. Where did your Christ come from? From God and a woman. Man had nothing to do with it."[9] God introduces his saving Son and saving way by circumventing the normal vehicles of power. Mary stands for the inconceivable in the male-dominated world, that the greatest source of power and change is not economics, war, politics, gender, ideology, or social forces, but a simple believer who says to God, "May it be to me as you have said."

Gabriel understands the trepidation with which Mary utters those words. The angel gives Mary a double assurance of God's faithfulness, an earthly assurance in Elizabeth, her barren kinswoman who became pregnant, and a heavenly assurance in the declaration, "For nothing is impossible with God." Much earlier in Israel's history a woman in a similar situation actually laughed when three strangers made the same promise. The angel's word to Mary, after all, is the very word that was spoken to Sarah in Genesis 18:14, which we considered in chapter 1. Both covenants, the Old and the New, were strangely conceived, to be sure. Both Sarah and Mary stood before the precious yet precarious choice that every believer faces, that God's promise is to be believed in spite of everything else. *Verbum Dei manet in aeternum*, said Luther—"God's word remains forever"—and we should "fear, love, and trust God above all things."[10]

"May it be to me as you have said." That is the best definition of faith in all the Bible, that we desire and permit God's word to become reality in our lives, "on earth as it is in heaven." Mary demands no outside proofs or signs that the impossible shall be made possible. She receives God's word in abandonment and trust, as the sole sufficiency for her life. For the first time in his conversation with humanity, God finds a worthy partner.

Some thirty years later a man prayed in lonely agony outside Jerusalem. As Jesus struggled with bearing the sins of humanity on a cross, he cried out, "Yet not what I will, but what you will" (Mark 14:36). This is essentially the same response as Mary's. Is it possible that Jesus learned it from his mother? We owe to Mary the only fitting response to the free and gracious call of God, "I am the Lord's servant."

QUESTIONS FOR DISCUSSION

1. What might Jesus' parents and location of his birth tell us about the way God works in our world?

2. How is it possible for a person to be morally virtuous yet a rebel against God?

3. What is the significance of artists portraying the annunciation of Mary by a beam from the angel to Mary's ear?

4. Read Exodus 40:34-35. How does God's "overshadowing" of the tabernacle in the wilderness prefigure the Holy Spirit's "overshadowing" of Mary in the annunciation?

5. After Mary said "Yes" to God's call, what comforted her through her journey . . . and gives us hope today?

7

Supreme Obedience

They went to a place called Gethsemane, and Jesus said to his disciples, "Sit here while I pray." He took Peter, James and John along with him, and he began to be deeply distressed and troubled. "My soul is overwhelmed with sorrow to the point of death," he said to them. "Stay here and keep watch."

Going a little farther, he fell to the ground and prayed that if possible the hour might pass from him. "Abba, Father," he said, "everything is possible for you. Take this cup from me. Yet not what I will, but what you will."

Then he returned to his disciples and found them sleeping. "Simon," he said to Peter, "are you asleep? Could you not keep watch for one hour? Watch and pray so that you will not fall into temptation. The spirit is willing, but the body is weak."

Once more he went away and prayed the same thing. When he came back, he again found them sleeping, because their eyes were heavy. They did not know what to say to him.

Returning the third time, he said to them, "Are you still sleeping and resting? Enough! The hour has come. Look, the Son of Man is betrayed into the hands of sinners. Rise! Let us go! Here comes my betrayer!"

—Mark 14:32-42

G. K. CHESTERTON ONCE said of Saint Francis of Assisi that he did not need to bear the stigmata (the marks of the cross) in his hands because he already bore them in his soul.[1] Chesterton's point was that martyrdom of the soul is the essential martyrdom, and that physical martyrdom, if it comes at all, is simply an expression of it. Thus, the decision behind a particular course of action is the source of the action, and is perhaps as difficult as (or more difficult than) the action itself. The initial movement in many things can be the hardest, whether writing an essay or biting the bullet and bailing out of a bad situation. Dante illustrates the force of this truth in *The Divine Comedy*. On his pilgrimage from hell to heaven, Dante stands at the foot of Mount Purgatory, despairing of reaching the summit. Virgil, Dante's guide, explains that the initial moves up the mountain are the most difficult, after which the ascent becomes easier. The Mount of Purgatory is a symbol of repentance, and the point of the allegory is that the desire to turn from sin to holiness is the hardest part of conversion; once that obstacle has been overcome, the remainder of the ascent becomes manageable and finally effortless.[2]

Not only can our inner decisions and battles be the most difficult of our experiences, they usually determine what we are and become. There is yet a further corollary to this truth: namely, that inner suffering, although hidden from outsiders and immeasurable in terms of cuts and bruises, can be more painful and more difficult to bear than physical suffering. Jesus' suffering in Gethsemane is a case in point. His agony in Gethsemane is the real prelude to the crucifixion. If the biblical accounts of Gethsemane and Golgotha are a basis by which to judge, Jesus' decision to allow God's will is more difficult than experiencing it, for his prayer of relinquishment is laden with more trauma and pathos than are the Roman nails themselves. In Gethsemane Jesus allows his soul to be crucified; on Golgotha he relinquishes his body.

Two things capture our attention in the Gethsemane story. The first is the magnitude of Jesus' suffering as he struggles with God's will. Jesus is fully aware of the ordeal before him and he desperately wants to be spared from it. He refers to the impending crucifixion as an "hour" and a "cup," both of which are metaphors for trials and suffering. We have seen that most characters in the Bible who are confronted with the will of God do not welcome it, but resist, attempt to exempt themselves, or even flee from it. Jesus is no exception. In fact, the effect of God's will on him is more traumatic than on any other person in the Bible: ". . . he began to be deeply distressed and troubled. 'My soul is overwhelmed with sorrow to the point of death. . . . Abba, Father,' he said, 'everything is possible for you. Take this cup from me.'" The original Greek behind this passage depicts the most excruciating suffering imaginable, and the word translated "deeply distressed" denotes suffering of alarming proportions. His grief is deep and overwhelming, "to the point of death." You will search the Bible in vain for anything approximating the suffering described here. Even David's heart-rending lament at the death of his son Absalom (2 Samuel 18:33) does not reach the depth of Jesus' agony. Jesus' soul is bent double in grief. Luke's account says that his agony resulted in sweat falling like drops of blood to the ground (Luke 22:44). In Hebrew, Gethsemane means "olive press," but it is Jesus himself who is pressed beyond human endurance.

It is worth considering why the specter of death haunts Jesus so. Surely we all know people who face death with less consternation and with greater bravery and composure than Jesus does. Why might that be? A popular answer, typical of Stoicism in Jesus' day as well as of Eastern philosophy in our own, is that his torment is the result of the failure to accept his circumstances in life. This school of thought asserts that the key to life is found in renouncing aspirations beyond one's reach and resigning oneself to one's allotted station in life.

The practical wisdom of this advice notwithstanding, Jesus' anguish is scarcely the result of disharmony with nature or an imbalance between his inner potential and outer circumstances. It is inconceivable that a man who had foretold his death on several occasions, who had put the most formidable opponents—both human and demonic—to rout, and who had never wavered in putting his call and the needs of others before himself should be afraid to do what every rogue and scoundrel since the beginning of time has done.

The truth is that the agony of Gethsemane is not due to the prospect of Jesus' own death. The issue in Gethsemane is not of a psychological or philosophical nature at all. It is theological. It has to do with God. God has ordained and sent Jesus to be the Sin-Bearer for all humanity. Jesus was clear about his mission on an earlier occasion when, on the way to Jerusalem, he spoke of his impending death as a "ransom for many" (Mark 10:45). A ransom is a payment surrendered to a second party for the release of a third party. In this instance, the ransom will be not a sum of money but Jesus himself, an innocent party surrendered for the benefit of a captive party. It is clear in Jesus' understanding that his betrayal, arrest, suffering, and inevitable death in Jerusalem are not a retribution for anything he has done. Nothing in his life warrants the ghastly pain, degradation, and shame of crucifixion. His death, rather, is a sacrifice to God, a ransom, that according to God's plan would have an atoning effect on others.

Nearly as remarkable as the ransom itself is the third party, "the others" for whom it will be rendered. Consider the people who have had something to do with Jesus in Jerusalem. His closest friends, both in physical proximity in Gethsemane as well as in sympathy with his mission, are Peter, James, and John. At the end of the Transfiguration Jesus had stood by all three of them at a crisis point in their faith. Now Jesus looks to the three to stand by him. In his darkest hour he asks them to "keep watch," but they fail him. The blessings of the Mount of Transfiguration were more agreeable to them than the demands of the Mount of Olives . . . not to mention the Mount of Calvary. The chosen three cannot stay awake, and Jesus is abandoned, like a scapegoat driven into the wilderness. He then prays to the Father, but the prayer is not granted.

Perhaps Jesus thinks of his Jewish kinsfolk. Had they not thrown their cloaks on the ground before him in a hero's welcome only a few days earlier? Had he not had compassion on them as "sheep without a shepherd" (Matthew 9:36)? Unfortunately, there will be no help from them; indeed, they will turn fiercely against him.

Perhaps Jesus thinks momentarily of the Romans. Could he not appeal to Roman law and justice in this crisis? But for Jesus, a mere pawn of political expediency, no reprieve will be granted from Rome.

And what about the general populace? In this one instance, might their shiftless sympathies be won for his rescue? But they, along with others, will cry out with venomous throats, "Crucify him! Crucify him!"

Abandoned by the world, Jesus turns again to the Father. Had not Isaac been rescued by God when Abraham was about to plunge the knife into his heart? If God had had mercy on the only son of Abraham, will he not have mercy on his only begotten Son? But God remains silent. With parched lips and outstretched arms Jesus will die with a cry of dereliction, "My God, my God, why have you forsaken me?" (Mark 15:34).

These are "the others,"—friends, disciples, fellow Jews, Romans—for whom Jesus will render his life as a ransom. Who among them is worthy of that ransom? Even the trusted few among them have betrayed him. The remainder are either indifferent or hostile. The apostle Paul grasped this scandalous reality with uncommon clarity. It was not for the worthy that Christ died, asserted Paul, but for outright "enemies" and "sinners" (Romans 5:8-10). Paul knew this truth firsthand, for his own life had been a scandal; the worst persecutor of the gospel had become its greatest herald. A poem by Dietrich Bonhoeffer captures the scandal as well. In reflecting on what Isaiah the prophet might have meant when he said that the "government would be on his shoulders" (Isaiah 9:6), Bonhoeffer wrote a poem called "God Is a God of Bearing":

> "And the government shall be upon his shoulder,"
> The government of the world is supposed to lie

on the weak shoulders of this newborn child!
One thing we know:
These shoulders will in any event get to carry
the burden of the entire world.
With the cross, all the sin and distress of this world
will be loaded onto these shoulders.
But the government will consist,
not in the bearer's breaking down under the burden,
but in his bringing it to the goal.[3]

It is a frightening thing to imagine what it will be like to bear the wrath of God against our own sins. But imagine what it would mean to suffer for every act of malice, pride, greed, selfishness, and hatred in history; for every war, plague, genocide, massacre, slaughter, siege, and famine in history; for every murderer, tyrant, thief, liar, cheat, coward, war criminal, and rapist in history. In some way that we cannot fathom, the burden and guilt of all human malevolence and evil is loaded onto Jesus' shoulders. And because Jesus is without sin and entirely undeserving of such a fate, in Jesus' own flesh God will do something by his death that will condemn and nullify all those sins.

The disciples, of course, cannot see this, nor have they the slightest inkling of the thunderstorm in Jesus' soul. If you and I could have been in Gethsemane that night we also would have been numb from the neck up. Even if we follow every word of the Gethsemane account, none of us can fathom Jesus' experience in this event. His anguish and sorrow and profound distress are due to his self-sacrifice for the wickedness of the human race. His suffering in this event is light years removed from us mortals because his holiness and his divine compassion are so unlike ours.

Let no one suppose that because Jesus is closer to God than we are that he suffers less than we do. Exactly the opposite is true, as a moment's reflection evinces: a child is more sensitive to evil than a dog, a virtuous person more than a child, and an angel more than a virtuous person. The Son of God likewise suffers evil, pain, and injustice more than an angel, more than every creature of God combined. It is this that weighs down the soul of Jesus and presses the blood of sacrifice from his all-compassionate heart. His colleagues trifle with drowsiness, but a battle is raging within the soul of our Lord that will determine the fate of the world.

The inner suffering of Jesus, incidentally, is not limited to Gethsemane. It also extends to Golgotha. It is remarkable with what reserve and decorum the New Testament describes the crucifixion of Jesus, the most ghastly and shameful form of execution. The apostle Paul, whose proclamation of the gospel centers on the cross of Christ (1 Corinthians 2:2), never indulges in the cruelties of crucifixion. The earliest Gospel, Mark, simply reports that "they crucified him" (Mark 15:24). No hammer blows, no blood and gore, no Hollywood close-ups. The avoidance of such details is not simply due to the fact that crucifixion was a horrible commonplace of Roman Palestine and needed no more elaboration at that time than gas chambers and firing squads do today. The refusal to indulge in graphic rehearsals of the crucifixion demonstrates that the New Testament does not want a decision of faith to be based on sentimentality, to be evoked by pity or wrung from us by a play on our emotions. What is stressed in the Gospel accounts, rather, is the mockery, scorn, ridicule, and humiliation that Jesus was subjected to on the cross. These, more than his physical suffering, reveal the true opposition and rejection that God experienced when he became one of us.

In Philippians 2:8, the apostle Paul reflected on the Incarnation—God's becoming a human being in Jesus of Nazareth—in these words:

> And being found in appearance as a man,
> he humbled himself and became obedient to death—
> even death on a cross!

When, exactly, did Jesus become "obedient to death"? Not at Golgotha, for by then he was a prisoner and no longer free to obey or not. He became obedient to death in the struggle at Gethsemane. There in the Kidron Valley, where Jesus is still free to take an exit ramp from his fate, he submits himself inescapably to God's will. And what happens in the mind and will of Jesus at that point is conclusive for what will happen to the whole world, nay to the vast reaches of interstellar space, for he has reconciled "to himself all things, whether things on earth or things in heaven" (Colossians 1:20). Apart from Gethsemane there can be no Golgotha. Golgotha, of course, claims far greater attention in the history of art and literature than does Gethsemane. The Middle Ages and Renaissance produced paintings on the crucifixion like we produce movies with sex and car chases and explosions. Paintings of Gethsemane are far fewer, but that is not because Gethsemane is less important. It is simply because it is easier to paint a cross than to paint a decision leading to a cross.

Not long ago I was talking with a woman who has known considerable hardship in life, including growing up in an abusive home and losing three siblings to cancer. The occasion of our conversation was her having lost her job. Nothing, she told me, compared to the pain of humiliation and shame she felt at losing her job—not even the deaths of her brothers and sisters. My experience and hers both had Gethsemane qualities to them: the inner battles were different from and more difficult than the obvious battles without.

The disciples simply see a man at prayer, agitated to be sure, but still only a man at prayer. You and I may see a person walking down the street or having a cup of coffee or telling a story at a party, an ordinary scene in an ordinary day. But the disciples cannot see into the heart of Jesus, nor can you and I see into the heart of another human being. In the prayer of Gethsemane, the salvation of the world is at stake; in our colleague's case, an eternal soul may be hovering between heaven and hell.

This, then, is the first truth of Gethsemane. Jesus' inner turmoil and suffering determine the accomplishment of God's will at Golgotha itself. In Gethsemane Jesus seals his mission to be the Savior of the world; at Golgotha he carries it out. There is, however, a second aspect of Gethsemane that is equally remarkable, and perhaps even more difficult to grasp. It is the sense of separation and loneliness that Jesus experiences as a result of his decision to obey God. "My God, My God," he cries, "why have you forsaken me?" How profoundly disturbing this final utterance of Jesus. How can it be that where Jesus most perfectly submits to God's will he feels most excluded from God's presence? Why does Jesus' obedience to God's will produce within him the experience of abandonment by God? And if this is true of the sinless Son of God, what might it mean for us? If we obey the will of God, might we forsake everything we ever wanted or hoped for?

Even a person of no religious inclination must be moved, even offended, by Jesus' final plea. Submission to God's will is rare enough in our egoistic and self-aggrandizing world. When a lonely soul finally does something altruistic and compassionate, is the reward abandonment? Do faith and obedience lead to exclusion from God? Could not Jesus have died, as did Socrates, with a sympathizing fellowship at his side? Even if no humans empathized, could not God have sustained Jesus in his tormented trials? The necessity of Jesus' suffering as Sin-Bearer we can perhaps understand, but not his abandonment by God. Job's plaintive cry echoes through Gethsemane:

> But if I go to the east, he is not there;
>   if I go to the west, I do not find him;
> When he is at work in the north, I do not see him;
>   when he turns to the south, I catch no glimpse of him.
> (Job 23:8-9)

We press the question as much from self-interest as from dismay at Jesus' suffering: will God abandon us in our ultimate trials, in our deepest longings, in the face of death?

Often, I believe, we avoid such questions, perhaps because we fear our irreverence in asking them, or even because we fear the more terrible possibility that the Bible or God himself cannot answer them. For many, superficial faith is safe faith. Listen, however, to the words of C. S. Lewis:

> I sometimes wonder if we have even begun to understand what is involved in the very concept of creation. If God will create, He will make something to be, and

yet to be not Himself. To be created is, in some sense, to
be ejected or separated. Can it be that the more perfect
the creature is, the further this separation must at some
point be pushed? It is saints, not common people, who
experience the "dark night." It is men and angels, not
beasts, who rebel. Inanimate matter sleeps in the bosom
of the Father. The "hiddenness" of God perhaps presses
most painfully on those who are in another way nearest
to Him, and therefore God Himself, made man, will of
all men be by God most forsaken?[4]

In the fifteenth century the German mystic Thomas à Kempis
anticipated Lewis: "When thou thinkest thyself farthest off from Me,
oftentimes I am nearest unto thee. When thou countest almost all to
be lost, then oftentimes the greatest gain of reward is close at hand."

Jesus' separation from God is not the result of a meaningless universe, or worse, of divine sadism, but of his very likeness
to God, his closeness and obedience to the Father. We have not
struck the bedrock of nothingness and absurdity as we had feared.
The enigma of Jesus' exclusion from the Father has yielded to a
profound and liberating truth. And what is true of Jesus is also
true of his followers. In the midst of our struggles and loss and
pain, when "the hiddenness of God presses most painfully on us,"
to quote Lewis, we may be closer to God than we imagine. It was
Luther who said:

> It is not a bad thing but a very good sign if the opposite of
> what we pray for appears to happen. This is so because the
> counsel and will of God far excel our counsel and will, as it
> says in Isa. 55:8: "For my thoughts are not your thoughts,
> neither are your ways my ways, says the Lord." Hence, it
> comes about that when we pray to God for something,
> whatever it may be, and he hears our prayers and is about
> to fulfill them, he does so in such a way that he contra-
> venes all our conceptions. God does all this because it is
> his nature first to destroy and bring to nothing whatever
> is in us before he gives us his own, as it is written: "The
> Lord makes poor and makes rich; he brings down to hell
> and brings back again" (1 Sam. 2:7,6). When, therefore,
> everything around us seems hopeless and all that happens

goes against our prayers and wishes, then those "groanings" commence "that cannot be uttered." And then "the Spirit helps us in our weakness . . . and intercedes for us with groans that words cannot express" (Rom. 8:26).[6]

Luther was right. God makes us weak so that we may be serviceable to his kingdom. God makes of us what we could not imagine; he assigns us to posts that we would never choose. He does this not to inflict pain on his servants, but to use them for greater purposes than they are capable of on their own. It is a divine mystery, like pruning: God cuts away so that something greater may appear. It happened to the Servant of the Lord in Isaiah, who lamented that his words and deeds, honed like a sharp sword and a swift arrow, remained unused by God. What seemed utter futility to the Servant, however, was used by God to bring his salvation not simply to Israel but to the ends of the earth (Isaiah 49:1-6). It happened to Jesus in Gethsemane, who prays to be spared, but whose death becomes the keystone in the master plan of God. It sometimes happens to ordinary people.

In 1940 the German army sealed off an 840-acre ghetto in the heart of Warsaw, capital of Poland. Among the 400,000 Jews who were crowded into the infamous Warsaw Ghetto was a man named Janusz Korczak. Korczak (pronounced KOR-shock) was a Jewish educator who wrote some fifteen books, both theoretical and practical, relating to early childhood education. He was also the director of an orphanage, and had been for nearly thirty years when the German forces invaded Poland. Korczak rescued hundreds of youngsters from the unspeakable misery of the Ghetto and attempted to protect them from deportation to death camps. In 1942 Korczak was informed that the two hundred children in his charge were to be shipped to the death camp of Treblinka. The children panicked. Korczak himself had not been included in the order, but he suppressed the truth and told the children they were going on a picnic in the country, and he went with them. In Treblinka the children were allowed to live with Korczak in a barrack. When the order came for "the showers," the children again panicked. Although the order again did not include Korczak, he knew that if he promised to go with the children that they would have the courage to face the unknown. At the door to the gas chamber Korczak refused a last-minute offer of his freedom, choosing instead to go with the children to their deaths.

At Yad Vashem, the museum and memorial to the Holocaust in Jerusalem, Korczak's heroism has been commemorated in a simple and haunting monument: a black monolith of a man's compassionate face — Janusz Korczak's — emerging from the faces of many children.

In Gethsemane, Jesus' face emerges from a panorama of faces as well, but they are not the faces of innocent children. They are the faces of Judas the betrayer; of Pontius Pilate, who caved in to political expediency rather than holding the fort of justice; of the Sanhedrin, with jaws set in religious pride; of the fickle and feckless crowd; of the lethargic and self-justifying disciples. If we care to look at such faces, we shall see our own among them. Jesus emerges from the prayerful agony of dark Gethsemane unwilling, like Korczak, to accept a personal reprieve. His face is set like flint to drink the "cup," to face the "hour," to give his life a ransom for many. "Everything is possible for you," prays Jesus to the Father. Everything is possible, that is, except one thing: a way around Golgotha, for apart from the cross the world cannot be saved from sin. Salvation is the one nonnegotiable thing for grace, for grace will not allow sin and death to be the final word. God will not allow the world to be lost. "Through [Christ] God has reconciled to himself all things, whether things on earth or things in heaven, by making peace through [Christ's] blood, shed on the cross" (Colossians 1:20).

Not allowing a thing to be lost. A neighbor of mine recently rescued a dog from an animal shelter. The dog responded to her overtures of love and care by gnawing on the furniture, chewing up the laundry, and digging holes in the yard. "What are you going to do?" I asked. She looked me straight in the eye and with steeled resolve said, "I am determined to save this creature from destruction and see it enjoy a life it has never known!" That is grace. We do everything imaginable to destroy ourselves, others around us,

GRACE

even the world itself. But the Son of God resolves in Gethsemane not to allow that to happen.

This brings us to the heart of God's redeeming intrusion into our world, to the saving mystery of the gospel. Throughout the conversations of this book we have been grappling with the depth of the divine condescension — that God, in his love for his errant creation, stoops to enter our broken world however possible — as three strangers visiting an aged Bedouin and his wife, as a man pursuing and wrestling with a scheming opportunist, as an angelic visitant to a man who recognizes oppression but cannot find the courage to fight it, as a voice from heaven to a Moses or Jonah or Mary. In these and other ways God has appeared among us. Already in the visitation of the three strangers to Abraham and Sarah we observed that these surprise and incognito intrusions are forerunners, intimations, anticipations of an ultimate intervention in the Incarnation. What God has done suggestively and sporadically and provisionally earlier in the divine drama, God does conclusively in Jesus of Nazareth.

And yet even the preliminary appearances and intrusions have not fully prepared us for the incarnation of Jesus, for in Jesus — and this is particularly evident in the suffering of Gethsemane — we are introduced to something entirely new and unprecedented, a final, once-for-all culmination of the divine intrusion into our world "in the fullness of time" (see Galatians 4:4). In Jesus of Nazareth we do not see yet another instance of God *among* us, but a total identification of God as one *of* us! Jesus is not simply another guise or semblance of God. Jesus is not another temporary mask of God breaking into the story of Israel to accomplish a finite task. When we see Jesus we do not see simply the effects of a divine intrusion; we see the Divine Intruder himself. In this man kneeling in agony in Gethsemane we see the human face of God, and through his sorrow and pain we hear the very heart of God become human. From his lonely agony we learn that God does not stand aloof from the pain inherent in creation but that he enters fully into it, takes it upon himself, accepts it deeper into his being than any human has ever done or could ever possibly do. Just as Janusz Korczak, refusing to accept a separate fate for himself, forsook his privileged status and effectively *became* a child, so too in Jesus God empties himself of his divine prerogatives and *becomes* a human being, a human being subjected to the utmost degradations of a Roman crucifixion.

When we understand the Incarnation we are enabled to hear Jesus' prayer in Gethsemane in a new way. Unlike the other conversations in this volume, the prayer of Gethsemane at first appears to be a monologue, for only the voice of Jesus is heard: "*Abba*, Father, everything is possible for you. Take this cup from me. Yet not what I will, but what you will." And yet this too is a conversation, for in the prayer of Gethsemane both the human and divine natures of Jesus are heard. In this prayer of supreme obedience, Jesus is speaking both as a human being *for* us and as God *to* us. Hoping to avoid the cross, the human nature cries out, "Take this cup from me." That is the human word, utterly transparent and honest, expressing the desperation and even resistance that characterize every human response to the intrusion of the divine will into our world. This word dispels every suspicion that God holds himself back or spares himself from the worst dregs of human experience. Jesus is not sheltered from the ravages of human existence but, even more than we, accepts the unmitigated consequences of them. "For [God] knows how we are formed, he remembers that we are dust" (Psalm 103:14). How completely Jesus' agony in Gethsemane fulfills that truth.

In the prayer of Gethsemane we hear the most profound voice of human experience, uncut and uncensored. But we also hear more than this human voice. We hear in this same Jesus the word of God, "*Abba*, Father, everything is possible for you." In Gethsemane we hear again God's word to Sarah and Mary — "For nothing is impossible with God" — the one word that God longs for humanity to hear and believe. But in Gethsemane it is not declared to Jesus as it was to Sarah and Mary, but to us *through* Jesus as God Incarnate. Fully accepting the truth of the all-possibility of God, Jesus utters the final word in which the human and divine unite in perfect submission within himself, the word that is his by nature and ours by faith: "Yet not what I will, but what you will."

QUESTIONS FOR DISCUSSION

1. Why is Jesus' decision to allow God's will in Gethsemane more difficult than experiencing it at Golgotha? Discuss the significance of this for discipleship.

2. Describe a time when an inner decision was more difficult than the outward experience.

3. What would keep you from praying Jesus' words in Gethsamane, "Not what I will, but what God wills"?

4. Has there ever been a time in your life when God seemed hidden from you, only to discover later that he was closer than you could have imagined?

5. How does Jesus' inner turmoil help us become more aware of the turmoil that others face? How does this affect our attitudes and actions toward others?

8

Converting the Converted

Meanwhile, Saul was still breathing out murderous threats against the Lord's disciples. He went to the high priest and asked him for letters to the synagogues in Damascus, so that if he found any there who belonged to the Way, whether men or women, he might take them as prisoners to Jerusalem. As he neared Damascus on his journey, suddenly a light from heaven flashed around him. He fell to the ground and heard a voice say to him, "Saul, Saul, why do you persecute me?"

"Who are you, Lord?" Saul asked.

"I am Jesus, whom you are persecuting," he replied. "Now get up and go into the city, and you will be told what you must do."

The men traveling with Saul stood there speechless; they heard the sound but did not see anyone. Saul got up from the ground, but when he opened his eyes he could see nothing. So they led him by the hand into Damascus. For three days he was blind, and did not eat or drink anything.

In Damascus there was a disciple named Ananias. The Lord called to him in a vision, "Ananias!"

"Yes, Lord," he answered.

The Lord told him, "Go to the house of Judas on Straight Street and ask for a man from Tarsus named Saul, for he is praying. In a vision he has seen a man named Ananias come and place his hands on him to restore his sight."

"Lord," Ananias answered, "I have heard many reports about this man and all the harm he has done to your saints in Jerusalem. And he has come here with authority from the chief priests to arrest all who call on your name."

But the Lord said to Ananias, "Go! This man is my chosen instrument to carry my name before the Gentiles and their kings and before the people of Israel. I will show him how much he must suffer for my name."

Then Ananias went to the house and entered it. Placing his hands on Saul, he said, "Brother Saul, the Lord—Jesus, who appeared to you on the road as you were coming here—has sent me so that you may see again and be filled with the Holy Spirit." Immediately, something like scales fell from Saul's eyes, and he could see again. He got up and was baptized, and after taking some food, he regained his strength.

—Acts 9:1-19

S AUL—BETTER KNOWN AS THE apostle Paul—is one of the most formative and influential characters in history. Not the least appealing aspect of his life is that he was a fierce opponent of the Way who became a staunch exponent of it. He was an accomplice in the killing of Stephen, the first Christian martyr, and this he followed with a campaign of terror, "ravaging the church like a wolf," to give the sense of the Greek (Acts 8:1-3). With sanction from the chief priest and the bile of a true believer, Saul resolved to do in Damascus what he had done in Jerusalem. His errand turned out to be one of the most remarkable ventures in history. The man who set out from Jerusalem on a war horse had to be led by hand into Damascus. The keen-eyed heresy hunter arrived at his goal blind. The partisan whose prime target had been to knock down the church was knocked off his own horse. The archpersecutor of the church had become its foremost champion. Such was the conversion of Saul, enemy-number-one of the faith.

But the story does not end there. Indeed, far from it. There is another conversion that must take place if God's purpose for Saul's life is to be realized. That is the conversion of the church in Damascus, as represented by Ananias. The ninth chapter of Acts is really about two conversions: one is the conversion of Saul, and the other is the conversion of the church to accept Saul. The first is the more dramatic, but the second is no less important for the fulfillment of God's plan.

Ananias is introduced simply as "a certain disciple in Damascus," according to the Greek (Acts 9:10). A disciple is commonly thought of as a follower or doer, but both the Hebrew and Greek roots of "disciple" in the Bible relate to *learning* as opposed to acting. In the New Testament a disciple is one who submits to learning the new life that God reveals to believers in Jesus Christ. It is hard to learn something well enough for it to change our lives. Learning the will of God is no exception, as Ananias is about to discover.

God appears to Ananias not unlike the way he appeared to Saul—in a vision, although in Ananias's case the appearance, at least initially, is less adversarial. "Ananias," says God, calling him by name. Like Moses, like Isaiah, like any number of the faithful, Ananias responds reverently and receptively: "Here I am." The divine–human encounter begins for Ananias as it does for others with an overture from God and a human response.

But the conversation immediately takes an unexpected turn. Ananias is instructed to get up and go out to Straight Street—a street that remains in Damascus to this day—and search out Saul of Tarsus, who is staying in the house of a man named Judas. Saul, he is told, is praying and has seen him—Ananias—in a vision coming to him and laying his hands on him so that he might receive his sight.

That God has already introduced Ananias in a vision to Saul as an agent of reconciliation is a statement of considerable consequence. Ananias, after all, has not been consulted about any such thing. Had he been, he would have fled like a cat from a bath. The announcement is rather like that of a man buying an engagement ring for a woman who detests him. Nor is there a hint of negotiation in the announcement; for example, *if* Ananias will go, *then* Saul can be restored. In repeating the vision of Saul to Ananias, God has, with sovereign freedom, revealed to Ananias what it means for Ananias to be the instrument of his will in this particular situation.

Most of us are familiar with the psychological distinction between the ideal self and the real self. The ideal self is the self we imagine ourselves to be, the self we desire to be, the self we project to the world and wish to be remembered. The real self, on the other hand, is what we actually are and do, some aspects of which deviate from the ideal self and are much less agreeable to us and others. The two selves might be pictured as two separate circles. Although no one's circles are concentric (with the exception of Jesus'), people are more or less integrated personalities depending on the overlap or distance between the two circles.

It appears that God has something corresponding to an ideal image of each Christian. The believer God sees is the redeemed person, fully transformed by and conformed to Jesus Christ (see Ephesians 4:13; 1 John 3:2). This explains why God addressed Gideon, as we recall from chapter 4, as a mighty warrior and man of valor when Gideon was still a timid dissident (Judges 6:12). As Christians, we are of course daily made aware of our unfinished state; we are very much like those uncompleted statues of Michelangelo whose figures are struggling to free themselves from their stone bondage. But God does not look on our present rough-hewn and inchoate state as either our true or final state. He sees rather what we are by faith and what we shall be in glory, true siblings of Jesus Christ (Romans 8:29). This certainly appears to be the case with Ananias, for the Ananias presented in the vision to Saul is a rather different Ananias from the one who is remonstrating with God.

The resistant Ananias keenly regrets having responded favorably to God in the first place. Ananias is not only incapable of seeing himself in the image projected by God, he is incapable of seeing Saul as anything other than a hater and hunter of Christians. Ananias's first response to God had been "Yes, Lord"; his second response, however, is "*But*, Lord!" Saul is an archenemy. He has hunted Christians, imprisoned Christians, killed Christians — and he is prepared to do the same to Christians in Damascus. These are not rumors; they are facts. Saul is no ally; he is an enemy. He has the church on the ropes. Saul is the reason Christians in Damascus are praying so fervently. "Deliver us from evil" means deliverance from Saul. The church wants to be saved from Saul, not sent to him! A rendezvous with Saul on Straight Street is a hornet's nest, and Ananias is in no mind to get stung.

Ananias's attitude is typical of the way the church often regards the Sauls of the world. The gospel, to be sure, is good news for sinners, but the church often looks like a club for the righteous. The gospel is intended for people of no reputation, but the church is full of people of good reputation. Compare the church to an Alcoholics Anonymous meeting, for example. At an AA meeting everyone admits to having a problem with drinking, but at church people try to look like they have it all together. There is almost no place where it is harder to share our faults, failings, and sins. You would never guess from observing a family at the coffee hour what happened in the car on the way to church.

When the church is uncomfortable with Saul it is uncomfortable with Christ, for Christ confronts Ananias in Saul. One of the repeated lessons we have learned from the divine–human conversations in this book is that God is not who Abraham and Sarah and Jacob and Mary think he is. And if they must learn anew who God really is, so must we. One of the sharpest critics of Christianity was Ludwig Feuerbach, the nineteenth-century Hegelian philosopher, who asserted that God was essentially a *Wünschbild*, a projection of the noblest human ideals onto an eternal canvas and baptized as "God." Simply put, Feuerbach believed that God was made in man's image, a human invention derived from our own needs and desires.[1] Although Feuerbach was an atheist desirous of discrediting and demolishing Christianity, there is at least a subliminal truth in his critique. In truth, we all — biblical characters notwithstanding — attempt to fashion God in our own likeness. Our values become God's values, our enemies become God's enemies. One of the reasons that God must and does intrude into our world is to prevent us from doing the very thing Feuerbach accuses us of doing, of making God in *our* image. The divine intrusions are thus correctives that redefine and preserve God's true nature, sovereign purposes, and infinite mercy. Nearly each character in this book must, in some degree, submit to such correctives. Hence, Christ appears to Ananias in the uncomfortable person of Saul in order to teach Ananias that the church is not his — or our — church, but Christ's church. Christ's purposes and ways in this world are never identical with human judgments; they exceed human judgments to the degree that God exceeds humanity.

Jesus' parables were also divine correctives, "tracer bullets" to the true (as opposed to false) God. One of his parables conveys the very truth that Ananias must learn, of God's unrecognized presence in the outcast and naked, the cold and hungry. The scene is the gathering of the nations for the Final Judgment. To those on his right the king says, "I was hungry and you fed me, thirsty and you gave me something to drink, a stranger and you invited me in, naked and you clothed me, sick and you looked after me, in prison and you visited me." To those on his left the king appeared likewise, but he was not fed or received or helped or visited. The response of the nations on both right and left is one of *surprise*, neither realizing that what they did — or failed to do — was done or not done to Jesus Christ. "Lord, when did we see you hungry or thirsty or a stranger or needing clothes or sick or in prison?" they ask. The king answers, Whatever you did to the least of these my brethren you did to me! (Matthew 25:31-46). Jesus manifests himself in unexpected individuals — the needy, outcasts, even adversaries. Our response to them is our response to Christ.

When Corrie and Betsie ten Boom were in the concentration camp of Ravensbrück they vowed that if they should survive the war they would travel the world and testify that God's love is greater than the deepest darkness. Betsie perished in Ravensbrück, and Corrie was left to fulfill the vow alone when she was miraculously released shortly before the end of the war. "Lord," she prayed, "I will go anywhere you send me, but not to Germany. I never want to hear a word of German again in my life." As we have learned from the conversations in this book, and as Corrie was about to learn, it is not advisable to tell God you will *never* do something. There is something in the divine temperament that finds such a statement an irresistible challenge. Two years later Corrie was speaking on a dangerous topic in a dangerous place: the topic was forgiveness, and the place was Munich, Germany. After the speech she was approached by a man whom she remembered as a guard who had mocked Betsie and her as they had stood naked at the processing center at Ravensbrück. "How grateful I am for your message, Fräulein," he said. "To think that Christ has washed my sins away." He reached out to shake Corrie's hand, but her arm was riveted to her side. Inside she was a cauldron of vengeance at what this man had done to her and countless others in a camp where 96,000 women and children were killed. She felt nothing, not the slightest spark of charity or forgiveness. At last she prayed, "Jesus, I cannot forgive him. Give me your forgiveness." Corrie extended her hand to the man. "From my shoulder along my arm and through my hand," she said, "a current seemed to pass from me to him, while into my heart sprang a love for this stranger that almost overwhelmed me. I discovered that it is not on our forgiveness any more than on our goodness that the world's healing hinges, but on His. When [God] tells us to love our enemies, He gives, along with the command, the love itself."[2]

If Corrie could not forgive this man, then God could not forgive her. The Lord's Prayer had taken on new meaning: "Forgive us our debts, *as we also have forgiven our debtors*" (Matthew 6:12, emphasis added). In this man, her enemy, Christ was standing before her.

Ananias's resistance is no less dogged. He rehearses the liturgy of Saul's malefactions. Like Corrie's memory of the prison guard, Ananias's report of Saul is fact. True as such facts and labels are, they can also be traps to those who rest secure in them. We easily accept them as the final truth about others, and this relieves us of further dealings with them. But the gospel offers no such relief. God is not finished with people when we are. Our world is mad over labels, like a petty bureaucrat with a rack of rubber stamps: liberals and conservatives, rightists and leftists, communists and free-marketers, cultists and Satanists, straights and gays, skinheads, Klansmen, eco-freaks, druggies. There is no end to our labels and categories. Some of these groups are indeed as hostile to the Christian faith as Saul once was. And all of them can become so if given final allegiance. But equally true, God has raised up from these and other groups extraordinary witnesses in our own time: Aleksandr Solzhenitsyn, a communist; Charles Colson, a rightist; Eldridge Cleaver, a leftist; Archbishop Romero, a conservative; Jacques Ellul, a liberal; Mortimer Adler, an atheist; Malcom Muggeridge, a pagan; Nicki Cruz, a drug dealer and killer. Are God's words to Ananias not also his words to us?

There is no rebuttal from God that Ananias has the facts wrong or that Saul's deeds are not so bad after all. Nor does God assuage Ananias's rancor. God hears Ananias out, but he does not accept the plea of the prosecution as the baseline of his will. "Go!" he commands. "This man is my chosen instrument. . . ."

How can Ananias's archenemy be God's "chosen instrument"? How can God call a man to his work who is intent on destroying it? Augustine tells a story from his own experience of how God answered a prayer by doing the *opposite* of what was prayed for. As a young man, Augustine desired to leave his home in North Africa to court the pleasures of life in Rome. His mother Monica, who longed for the salvation of her vain and worldly son, and who believed that Rome would further corrupt him, prayed fervently that Augustine would remain at home. Heedless of his mother's desires, Augustine

> sailed away, leaving her alone to her tears and her prayers. And what did she beg of you, my God, with all those tears, if not that you would prevent me from sailing. But you did not do as she asked you then. Instead, in the depth of your wisdom, you granted the wish that was closest to her heart. . . . The next morning she was wild with grief, pouring her sighs and sorrows in your ear, because she thought you had not listened to her prayer. But you were letting my own desires carry me away on a journey that was to put an end to those same desires, and you used her too jealous love for her son as a scourge of sorrow for her just punishment.[3]

The paradox of grace. It was in Italy that Augustine would meet the wise and godly Ambrose, bishop of Milan, under whom he would at last confess the faith he had long forsaken. "But you did not do as she asked you then. Instead, in the depth of your wisdom, you granted the wish that was closest to her heart." God denies Monica's prayer in order to grant her desire! God chooses a man whom the church loathes in order to do what the church loves.

The Divine Intruder, as we have seen, does not instruct his agents in the global strategy of his plan, but rather operates on a "need to know" basis. It is enough if a given individual can be won from opponent to partner and made serviceable for a particular aspect of the plan. The conversation, likewise, normally focuses on the segment of the race that God expects each human partner to run. In the conversation with Ananias, however, God elaborates his plan more than usual, particularly with regard to Saul. Saul, Ananias is informed, is God's "chosen instrument"; he will bear God's name before the leaders of Jews and Gentiles alike; and he must suffer much for God's name. God does not owe this elaboration to Ananias. If God is sovereign, he owes no justification of his actions to his creation any more than a potter, to cite an illustration of the apostle Paul, owes an explanation why he has made a lump of clay into a particular pot (Romans 9:20-21). God includes the overview of Saul's mission in the call of Ananias not because he owes him a justification, but because he does not desire Ananias to be a mindless cog, a grunt laborer with no knowledge and no "ownership" in the divine work to which he is called. Ananias is a partner, not a lackey, and partnership means seeing enough of the field of play so that one shares the game and goal with others. God's dealing of us obstreperous human beings into the master plan of his will is a testimony to both his humility and his grace. An adult who parents a child from reason, explanation, partnership, and intentionality is a much better parent than one who plays only the ace of power. God is like the former parent. God holds cards in his hand that he has yet to play, and he divulges one of them in the game plan for Saul.

What God divulges of Saul aids Ananias in his acceptance of God's call to him. Ananias can go to Saul knowing that Saul too is subject to the sovereign authority and grace of God. Saul is no longer an opponent, but, by God's grace, a member of the body of Christ. Ananias understands this and does what God commands: he gets up, goes to Straight Street, and in one of the longest and most magnanimous reaches in history, extends the hands of grace to broken Saul. And what does he call him? The labels, the fears, the excuses — they are gone. "Brother Saul," he calls him. Christianity owes more to that reach and that address than it will ever know.

"No eye has seen, no ear has heard, no mind has conceived what God has prepared for those who love him" (1 Corinthians 2:9). God's ways are not our ways. The past is not always prelude.

The way things are is not the way they always must be. God is at work in our world as he was in the biblical world as a "fifth column," changing the outcome of the contest in the most unimaginable ways. The Divine Intruder will not allow the hardened human heart to become the measure of all things. He is making all things new, and the future is full of surprises.

Wilmer McLean was a farmer in the Shenandoah Valley in 1861. In the spring of that year two powerful armies met on his property—the Union army under General McDowell and the Confederate army under General Beauregard. The bloodiest war in American history began at Bull Run, a creek that ran through McLean's property. McLean was not at all sure why the armies were fighting, but he was quite sure he did not want them fighting on his small property. If he could not change the course of the war, he at least did not have to be part of it. McLean decided to sell out and go where the war would never find him. He chose the most obscure place in the whole country—or so he thought: an old house in the village of Appomattox Court House, Virginia. Four years later General Grant was pursuing General Lee through Virginia. In Appomattox County, Grant sent a message to Lee asking him to meet and sign a truce. The place where they met to sign the peace that ended the Civil War was Wilmer McLean's living room.[4]

There is no escaping the call of God. We may, like Augustine, secretly desire to follow God's will, "but not yet." We may, like Francis Thompson, "flee him down the labyrinthine ways" of our own devices and desires. Perhaps, like Abraham and Sarah, long years of waiting have left us despairing of God; or perhaps, like Jonah or Ananias, it is not the absence of God but his outrageous demands that confound us. Whoever we are, wherever we are, God breaks into our lives in ways distinctive to each of us, calling, convicting, wooing, waiting to bring us to himself and to use us in unimaginable ways for his eternal purposes. God intrudes and interrupts not because he is boorish or tyrannical, but because our world is bent and proud and willful, and our hearts—yours and mine—are hardened to him. If he did not intrude we would not hear him and know him, and God cannot allow the world to persist in rebellion without being confronted, despite itself, with the conspiracy of grace. And God prevails in our world not because he is a divine autocrat whose will is raw power, but because if we and the world were left to ourselves we would all, despite our best intentions, refashion God in our own image and change the gospel of Jesus Christ into something other and less than it is, defacing and destroying the only true hope the world knows. God does not will that sin and rebellion be the last and final truth of the universe, but that the world, conceived in the wisdom and compassion of the Creator, would by the persistence of grace meet the God from whom it flees and for whom it longs.

QUESTIONS FOR DISCUSSION

1. Why do you think God used Ananias in Saul's life rather than someone else?

2. Why do you think church is a hard place to share our faults, failings, and sins?

3. Augustine said of his mother's prayer, "God did not do as she asked. Instead, in the depth of his wisdom, he granted the wish that was closest to her heart." What does this tell you about the way God answers prayer?

4. In the eight chapters of this book, what is the phrase that God keeps repeating to each character, and to us?

5. What insight, principle, or observation did you find most fresh, eye opening, or troubling in this book?

Notes

INTRODUCTION

1. Martin Buber, *I and Thou*, trans. W. Kaufmann (New York: Scribner's, 1970).

2. Dante, *The Paradiso*, canto 33, lines 116 and following.

CHAPTER ONE

1. Eleanor Lansing Dulles, *Berlin—The Wall Is Not Forever* (Chapel Hill: University of North Carolina Press, 1967), p. ix.

CHAPTER TWO

1. Augustine, *Confessions*, trans. R. S. Pine-Coffin, bk. 1, chap. 1.

2. Augustine, bk. 8, chap. 11.

3. Augustine, bk. 5, chap. 1.

CHAPTER THREE

1. Dietrich Bonhoeffer, "Wer Bin Ich?" in *Widerstand und Ergebung. Briefe und Aufzeichnungen aus der Haft*, herausgegeben von E. Bethge (München: Christian Kaiser Verlag, 1961), pp. 242-243 (my translation). An English version appears in Dietrich Bonhoeffer, *Letters and Papers from Prison*, rev. ed.,

ed. E. Bethge, trans. R. Fuller (New York: Macmillan, 1967), pp. 188-189.

2. Helmut Thielicke, *I Believe. The Christian's Creed*, trans. J. Doberstein and H. Anderson (Philadelphia: Fortress Press, 1968), p. 33.

3. C. S. Lewis, "The Unwelcome Fellow Traveler," chap. 11 in *The Horse and His Boy* (Scholastic Inc., 1988).

CHAPTER FOUR

1. See Peter Brown, *The Body and Society: Men, Women, and Sexual Renunciation in Early Christianity* (New York: Columbia University Press, 1988), pp. 165-66.

2. Corrie ten Boom, *In Ihm Geborgen: Meine Lebensgeschichte* (Wuppertal: Brockhaus Verlag, 1969), p. 5 (my translation).

3. Karl Barth, *The Epistle to the Romans*, 6th ed., trans. E. Hoskyns (New York: Oxford University Press, 1976), pp. 33-34.

4. See, "A Pencil in the Hand of God," *Time*, December 4, 1989, p. 11.

CHAPTER FIVE

1. C. S. Lewis, Surprised by *Joy: The Shape of My Early Life* (New York: Harcourt, Brace & World, 1955), pp. 228-229.

2. For an account of Assyrian atrocities, see Erika Bleibtreu, "Grisly Assyrian Record of Torture and Death," *Biblical Archaeology Review* 17 (January/February 1991), pp. 52-61.

3. Francis Thompson, The Hound of Heaven, in *The Golden Treasury*. Selected from the best songs and lyrical poems in the English language, ed. Francis T. Palgrave (New York: Macmillan, 1960), pp. 540-545.

4. The man who set out to disprove the resurrection was Albert H. Ross, who wrote under the pseudonym of Frank Morison, *Who Moved the Stone?* (London: Faber and Faber Limited, 1966).

5. Jon Krakauer, *Into Thin Air* (New York: Villard Press, 1997), pp. 240-241.

CHAPTER SIX

1. Dietrich Bonhoeffer, *The Mystery of Holy Night*, ed. M. Weber, trans. P. Heinegg (New York: Crossroad Publishing Company, n.d.), p. 8.

2. Eduard Schweizer, *Das Evangelium nach Markus* (Göttingen: Vandenhoeck & Ruprecht, 1968), p. 98 (my translation). For English version, see Eduard Schweizer, *The Good News According to Mark*, trans. D. Madvig (Atlanta: John Knox Press, 1970), p. 174.

3. *Quran*, Surah 3. Surah 19, entitled "Mary," also speaks of Mary.

4. John Milton, *Paradise Lost*, bk. 10, lines 979-991.

5. St. Bernard, Homilies 4, 8-9, *Opera Omnia* (Cistercian Edition 4, 1966), pp. 53-54. I thank Patricia Klein for this reference.

6. See Suetonius, *Lives of the Caesars*, Book III, "Tiberius," chaps. 43-44, in Suetonius, Volume I, trans. J. Rolfe, intro. K. Bradley, Loeb Classical Library, vol. 31 (Cambridge: Harvard University Press, 1998), pp. 371-375.

7. For Kierkegaard's discussion of the teleological suspension of the ethical, see *Fear and Trembling*, trans. W. Lowrie (Princeton: Princeton University Press, 1974), pp. 64-71 (Problem I).

8. See Dietrich Bonhoffer, *Ethics*, trans. E. Bethge (New York: Macmillan, 1965), pp. 240-241.

9. Sojourner Truth, *An Advent Sourcebook* (Chicago: Liturgical Training Publications), p. 54. I thank Patricia Klein for this reference.

10. That "we should fear, love, and trust God above all things" in life and death is repeated in each of Martin Luther's explanations of the Ten Commandments in his *Small Catechism* (1529).

CHAPTER SEVEN

1. G. K. Chesterton, *St. Francis of Assisi* (Garden Grove: Doubleday & Company [Image Books], 1957), p. 131.

2. Dante, *The Purgatorio*, canto IV.

3. Dietrich Bonhoeffer, *The Mystery of Holy Night*, p. 31.

4. C. S. Lewis, *Letters to Malcolm: Chiefly on Prayer* (New York: Harcourt Brace Jovanovich, 1964), p. 44.

5. Thomas à Kempis, *Of the Imitation of Christ* (New Canaan, Conn.: Keats Publishing, 1973), chap. 30, section 3.

6. Martin Luther, *Luther: Lectures on Romans*, ed. W. Pauck, vol. 15, The Library of Christian Classics (Philadelphia: Westminster Press, 1961), pp. 240-241.

CHAPTER EIGHT

1. Ludwig Feuerbach, *The Essence of Christianity*, trans. George Eliot, 1854.

2. Corrie ten Boom and John and Elizabeth Sherrill, *The Hiding Place* (Washington Depot: Chosen Books, 1971), p. 215.

3. Augustine, *Confessions*, bk. 5, chap. 8.

4. See Bruce Caton, *This Hallowed Ground* (New York: Pocket Cardinal Books, 1964), p. 476.

About the Author

JAMES R. EDWARDS IS Bruner-Welch Professor Emeritus of Theology at Whitworth University in Spokane, Washington. He holds degrees from Whitworth (B.A.), Princeton Theological Seminary (M.Div.), and Fuller Theological Seminary (Ph.D.). He has studied further at the University of Ziirich in Switzerland, the University of Tiibingen in Germany, Tyndale House in Cambridge, England, and the Center of Theological Inquiry in Princeton, New Jersey. He has traveled extensively in Europe, including former East Bloc countries, and in Israel, Turkey, and Greece. He has also been a translation consultant for Wycliffe Bible Translators in Colombia. Edwards has published several New Testament commentaries and numerous articles in scholarly and popular journals. His book Is *Jesus the Only Savior* (Eerdmans) was named Book of the Year in 2006 by Christianity Today. He was a pastor in Colorado Springs, where he was born and raised, and for nearly forty years he taught Bible, Biblical languages, and church history at the University of Jamestown (North Dakota) and Whitworth University. He is married and has two grown children and five grandchildren.

63014087R00082

Made in the USA
Lexington, KY
24 April 2017